IN QUEST OF GOLD

The break for the tape is on! The 1500-meter final 200 yards—
Olympic Trials, 1972.

IN QUEST OF GOLD

THE JIM RYUN STORY

Jim Ryun with Mike Phillips

1817

Harper & Row, Publishers, San Francisco
Cambridge, Hagerstown, New York, Philadelphia
London, Mexico City, São Paulo
Singapore, Sydney

Photos on pp. 110, 160, 161, 209, 212 from Jim Ryun's collection; p. 57 by George Long; p. 109 by Paul Petersen; p. 113 by Dan Poush, *Star-Free Press*; all other photos copyright © by Rich Clarkson.

FIRST EDITION

Designer: Jim Mennick

Library of Congress Cataloging in Publication Data

Ryun, Jim, DATE
  IN QUEST OF GOLD

  Includes index.
  1. Ryun, Jim, DATE   . 2. Runners (Sports)—
United States—Biography. I. Phillips, Mike, DATE
II. Title.
GV1061.15.R98A37   1984   796.4'26'0924 [P] 84-9080
ISBN 0-06-067021-5

84 85 86 87 88 10 9 8 7 6 5 4 3 2 1

Contents

Preface by *Mike Phillips*

As a mediocre high school middle-distance runner I paid little heed to the national track scene. However, as my collegiate performances began to improve and running became a serious part of my life, I became more keenly aware of track and field at the international level.

It was the mid-1960s. At that time a lanky, introverted miler from the Midwest *was* American running. He was accomplishing things on the track that no one had before, and it was only natural I would follow his career closely.

Thus Jim Ryun became for me—as he was for so many thousands—an idol, a folk hero, a symbol of what we all longed to be. I envisioned myself steadily improving to the point where someday we would finish a mile race side-by-side in a dead-heat sprint toward the tape. Of course, alongside Jim Ryun at that time I might as well have been a five-minute miler. And when an ailment forced my middle-distance days to an early conclusion, there was no choice but to abandon that dream.

But Jim Ryun never left my mind.

Initially my fascination had been with Jim Ryun the runner; his times and achievements were the focus of my attention. I analyzed the history of mile racing and accumulated a large file of clippings, photos, and statistics. I drew charts and graphs, compared dirt track times and other competitive factors, rated record performances, and ranked the great milers and 1500-meter runners of the last century according to a wide variety of parameters.

But as the career of Jim Ryun the runner went through its many ups and downs and eventually came to an end, I could not escape the notion that there was more to this man than I could ever realize by dissecting his achievements. My preoccupation with his exploits on the track was gradually replaced with an interest in his growth as a person. I sensed that he was someone who had matured through the years; a celebrity in the public spotlight whose personal and family integrity remained solid, he demonstrated a unique quality of life.

"Are these perceptions accurate?" I wondered. "Is there something distinctive about this man, apart from Jim Ryun the famous athlete?"

Part of my curiosity stemmed, no doubt, from the fact that I related to Ryun's timidity. We were the same age and competed in the same events. He was quiet, polite, no brash egotist. His very shyness before the press appealed to me.

"What really makes him tick?" I could not help but ask.

The men and women of the media covered his times and races and performances. But try as they might, it seemed they could never reveal the *real* Jim Ryun. His reticent personality and their consuming interest in athletic performance didn't mix. The press just never seemed to really *know* him.

Meanwhile, my own life progressed. My family and business and writing career grew. But always in the back of my mind lingered the sense of mystery surrounding Jim Ryun. I continued to be drawn to him, still wanting to know if my gut instincts about the quality of life he seemed to demonstrate were valid.

He was rarely in the news by this time. For several years I scarcely heard a whisper about him. Yet a small voice inside kept speaking to me: "Someday you will meet him. . . . You *must* get to know this man."

That voice grew stronger and stronger until it eventually suggested, "You've done a sizable amount of writing by now. Why don't you write a book on Jim Ryun's life?"

I took the suggestion seriously; I composed a letter and, after a look through one of the many telephone directories at our local library for his address, sent it off.

"Dear Jim," I said, in essence. "You don't know me, but I am a runner and a writer and I would be interested in writing your biography."

It was an admittedly forward way to begin a relationship. But the thirst to resolve the enigma Jim Ryun had long been for me could not be quenched short of taking such an action. And out of that beginning developed a correspondence that ultimately led to a close friendship with Jim Ryun and his family. For three years we exchanged letters and thoughts sporadically. Unknown to me, Jim

had already been making plans for a book that had not yet material-
ized for lack of an author.

Our letters increased in frequency, and we arranged to meet at
a 10K road race. At that time we and our wives became acquainted,
and we were able to discuss in more specific detail the book we
wanted to write. Several months later, in November of 1982, I
found myself driving over the Rockies from my home in California
to spend a month living with the Ryun family in Kansas. Soon I was
typing day and night to piece together the first draft of what would
eventually become *In Quest of Gold.*

You really get to know people when you eat with them, run
through mud and rain with them, suffer through leaky roofs and
zero-degree cold with them, when you watch TV with them and
play with their children and go to church and pray and laugh with
them, when you knock on their bedroom door at 7:30 in the morning to clear up a point in the manuscript, when you interview and
cross-examine them until tears are flowing and voices are heated.

Jim and Anne Ryun, together with their children, became more
than an abstract "project" that I had to write about. They became
intimate friends whom I grew to love.

Putting this book together was far from an easy assignment—
for any of us. The intense probing of my questions often forced Jim
and Anne to relive what had been painful and agonizing times. In
attempting to find a flow and order to the story of their lives, we
had to ask questions about their past that they had never confronted. Frustrations and disagreements were voiced. Tears were
shed. By the time we were through I had been taken so intimately
into Jim and Anne's memories of the events of their life together
that it was almost as though I had lived through it with them.

Thus the writing of the book itself became a learning and growing and broadening experience for each of us. Compiling the manuscript, revising the drafts, adding and deleting, became almost sec-
ondary to the knitting together of the bonds of friendship between
us. Yet the book had, from the beginning, been the thing that had
brought us together; and it therefore grew out of that relationship
and became even more a labor of love.

My original desire to find out "what makes Jim Ryun tick" was
certainly fulfilled beyond my expectations. The lives of Jim and
Anne Ryun have touched me, and I will always be richer for the

exposure. I went to Kansas to learn about this man who had fas-
cinated me, and I discovered that my intuitions about him had been
well founded.

When the initial month of writing was completed, my wife,
Judy, and youngest son, Gregory, flew to Kansas to make the drive
home to California with me. We were able to spend several additional days with the Ryuns, sharing as families rather than simply
writing a book. When we drove away we left not Jim Ryun the
celebrity, but Jim, Anne, Catharine, Drew, Heather, and Ned—our
good friends.

The draft of the book so hastily assembled during that month
in Kansas was but the beginning. From there it took many phone
calls and letters, taped questions and answers, several rewrites,
guidance from our editor, Roy M. Carlisle, of Harper & Row San
Francisco and great patience and trust from each of us toward all the
others involved to eventually see this book to completion.

Yet somehow all this "background" does not really tell you how
and why this book came to be written. Neither does Jim's fame as
an athlete, nor whatever skill I may or may not possess as a writer.
The telling ingredient in the story of this book itself, and in the
story of Jim Ryun's life, is a very personal quality found rarely in
today's world. Simply put, it is the quality of openness. Without
openness and honesty this book could never have been written.
Indeed, without them there would have been no story to tell.

Jim is a transparent man. What you see before you is the real
person. Rarely have I met an individual so free of hidden motive or
design, so unassuming, so willing to honestly lay before the world
the complete, unvarnished reality of who he is. Subtly putting on
airs is a duplicity absolutely unknown to him. He and his wife
welcomed me graciously into their home, and not once during my
visit did I pick up so much as the faintest hint that anyone was
trying to impress me. We talked about world records and unbelievable athletic accomplishments—but without a trace of boasting or
of mock humility.

I know that the same guileless transparency follows him when
he speaks at running clinics, appears on talk shows, visits the White
House, or rubs shoulders with the local farmers in a neighborhood
cafe. He is who he is, whether talking with the significant leaders
of our generation or chatting with a neighbor about the weather.

But I found this quality not only in Jim, but also in Anne.

Although she is vastly different than he, she shares his transparent openness. Jim's and Anne's lives mesh together; their personalities enrich one another. The original driving force prompting me to do this book came from Jim himself, but I received the added bonus of getting to know each one of the family in a personal way. Jim Ryun the runner can no longer be considered a separate entity from his family, from his deep friendship with his wife. Each family member is shaped by his or her relationships with the others.

Jim and Anne have their blind spots, as we all do; they have both strengths and weaknesses. Yet those very blind spots, and the Ryuns' willingness to confront them, provide the framework for a maturing process of daily growth.

The Ryuns are—well, they're simply *real* people. I write these words, therefore, with a heart full of appreciation for the openness I have witnessed in them. In telling this story, Jim did not try to make of life a solid series of "ups" by glossing over difficulties and hiding faults; rather, he showed a willingness to reveal the "downside" as well. The reality and forthrightness of his character have had a profound impact on me.

And that is the essence of the story that follows.

MIKE PHILLIPS
Eureka, California

Acknowledgments

No book comes into print by the efforts of its author alone. People and situations through the years work in different ways to mold us, mature us, and provide a framework for growth and development. Those who affix their name onto a title page recognize that they are but the final link in a lengthy progression of many who—consciously and unconsciously—played a role in bringing a certain story or group of ideas into print.

Jim and I are both keenly aware of the impact others have had on us, most of whom it would be impossible to mention in this brief allotted space. Several, however, stand out as having contributed to this book in specific ways. There is Len Lesourd of Chosen Books, who first instilled in Jim the vision for telling his story. Len's gracious flexibility as the actual publication moved into other hands provided a further boost to the project. I would like to acknowledge my co-worker Clarence Nason, who helped me along the way by reading the manuscript, offering suggestions, and taking many details off my shoulders, allowing me time to sit at my typewriter. We certainly owe a debt of gratitude to Rich Clarkson of the *Denver Post,* who has chronicled Jim's career in pictures since its earliest beginnings. His cooperation in the photographic side of production has been a vital asset.

As the manuscript entered the editorial process at Harper & Row, I came to appreciate deeply the profound responsibility an editor carries. Our editor at Harper & Row San Francisco, Roy M. Carlisle, was able to take a rough manuscript and our very nebulous notions about where the book should go and reduce them to their simplest terms. As I began the process of rewriting, Roy pointed me where we needed to go, crucified my pages with his awful red pen, and kept guiding and encouraging until we could see the thread of the story he had been confident of all along. Indeed, this book carries his stamp and is greatly a product of his editorial instincts and vision.

Our families, of course, have been a part of this project in many ways. Our wives, Judy and Anne, have offered detailed ideas, helpful criticism, boundless encouragement, and very practical and useful suggestions. Our children have been patient with us during the time we have necessarily had to take from them in order to complete what we set out to do.

To these and innumerable others who are bound up in our lives and who have thus helped shape this book—to you all, we are most grateful.

—MIKE PHILLIPS

I am also deeply indebted to those many other people who helped make this book a reality:

To Mike Phillips, his wife, Judy, and their sons, Robin, Patrick, and Gregory. As with any project of this dimension, it took everyone's cooperation and sacrifice. This is always especially true at the family level.

I appreciate Mike for the importunity he displayed in getting this book ready. Several years ago he had the vision and desire to write this book. The project had to be tabled at that time—Anne and I did not feel we had anything to share that would help people become all God wanted them to be—yet Mike persevered with follow-up letters, and eventually the time was right. I appreciate him and am so grateful for his endurance during this project.

To my family—my wife, Anne, and our four children, Heather, Catharine, Ned, and Drew—for their love, encouragement, and understanding of the time spent in compiling this book.

And to Roy M. Carlisle, our editor at Harper & Row San Francisco, for his unwavering devotion to seeing this book completed.

I thank you all.

—JIM RYUN

A Note from *Jim Ryun*

My good friend and fellow Kansas University track teammate Jim Olson stood in the driveway outside our Topeka duplex, exclaiming with his typical enthusiasm, "That's it, that's it! We'll title your book 'In Quest of Gold.' Get it, Jim? The book will follow your travels, your goals, your age-old desire to win a gold medal." That was the summer of 1971—years ago, thousands of miles ago.

God has plans for us that we, as people seemingly charting our own course, know not of. God longingly desires for us to turn to Him, to seek His ways above our own ways. Why, I asked myself, is God so persistent to have things His way? I have found the answer to be a simple one—His ways are *the best.*

And so, on my journey in quest of *my* gold medal, I met up with the God of this universe. How, in the midst of my track-oriented life, did this happen? Why is it of any interest to you?

Just prior to the 1972 Munich Olympics, my brother-in-law, Hank, wrote me a letter of encouragement. In it he expressed his lack of words for such a time as this: "I know that anything I do say now is only words, and words are a lot easier to form than the actions they symbolize." Hank was so right—without action, words are empty and life is empty.

So here I am thirteen years later with a book filled with words —words that certainly express, expound, explain the life I have lived. Words that would be empty if it were not for the very fact that they have required action. Life is action, and all of life requires unceasing action. Life is always changing, constantly in motion. It never stands still.

So it has been in my life—I have not stood still but rather sincerely sought after life. I have found that life to be in the very person of Jesus Christ, who said He was "the way, the truth, and the life." Oh, I am not about to say that I wasn't "living" without Jesus. I had certainly been born and was physically living, up to age twenty-five . . . my world records confirm this. I was alive and kicking, literally.

Then when I was twenty-five, I died. The old Jim Ryun was put to death and Jesus began a new life within me. I began living not just physically but mentally and spiritually as well, living the way God meant for me to live. My hope and prayer is that this book of words will encourage you to action in your own life, to action in accordance with God's will for you.

Of course, none of this would have been possible without much love and understanding from others. Second to Jesus Christ, my wife, Anne, has been my strongest supporter. Following our marriage, she lovingly assumed the role of Mrs. Jim Ryun, only to discover that running and its demands were something she had little preparation for. But she never gave up on me and continued to dream with me about a gold medal.

I've often wondered what a different life I might have led had I not been present at my sophomore orientation assembly and listened to coach Bob Timmons talk about running or what might have happened had Bob and Pat, his wife, not had me stay in their home during the summer months of 1964 before the U.S. Olympic team was selected?

My thanks go to the Lord, my wife, Bob and Pat Timmons, and many others like them who helped make this story about my life possible.

Prologue

The day was warm despite the sun's intermittent disappearances behind the scattered clouds. Beneath the radiant blue sky, the waters of the Pacific glistened less than two hundred feet away. Most of the more than four hundred bright and thinly clad runners of all ages had by now congregated at the park bordering Goleta Beach in Santa Barbara and were awaiting what for many would prove the highlight of the day. Nearly all had run ten-kilometer races before. America's road-running boom of the '70s had swept them along on its crest. But something about this 10K run on this particular day was unique. Some had driven great distances to be here, but not just for the race. This was the chance to see, run with, listen to, and—if luck was with you—maybe even meet a legend.

After another ten minutes of milling around, pulling on dry sweats, comparing times, and recounting details of the race, a gradual hush descended and heads began to turn toward the platform. "There he is," whispered a father to his son. "He used to be the greatest runner in the world—the man who broke Jazy's, Snell's, and Elliott's records."

Ascending the steps behind two others was a conspicuous young man in his mid-thirties, nearly 6'3", lean and handsome. He was dressed in a blue running suit, moved with poise and confidence, and replete with Southern California tan and windblown brown hair, he represented a commanding figure indeed.

"We thank you all for coming to participate with us in this run," began the announcer in charge of postrace activities. "I know you're anxious to get the awards over with so you can hear from our guest today. Without further delay then, I want to introduce you to the man I know you're already very familiar with, an athlete who participated in eight world-record-breaking runs. Three-time Olympian, Jim Ryun."

The tall Ryun stood amid scattered applause, took the microphone, flashed a smile, and said, "I'm so glad to be here. But I really do have to clarify that introduction. A couple of those world records I only coheld as a member of relay teams, the indoor mile mark I only tied, and the indoor half-mile record was never ratified. So the number eight represents a bit of an overstatement. But let's get on with the presentations."

For the next thirty minutes those on the podium announced and distributed the age-group awards for the completed race, Ryun shaking hands with each placer and joking amiably with contestants and crowd. His friendly and relaxed manner, so uncharacteristic of the Jim Ryun once known to the public as an athlete who avoided media contact and speaking engagements, was infectious. Everyone seemed to be having a good time.

When the award ceremony was completed, the race director stepped forward to say, "I know many of you athletes have come especially to participate in Jim's running clinic and we'd like to begin now by giving you the opportunity to listen to Jim share briefly and perhaps answer questions you might have. So right now I'd like to turn the mike back over to him."

"Thank you. I would like to respond to some of your questions. But first, if I may, I'd like to introduce my family. My wife Anne many of you probably know as she accompanies me to many races and other functions. We've been fortunate this time to bring along our daughter Heather who is fourteen, our sons Drew and Ned, eleven, and Catharine, nine."

There was a pause while Mrs. Ryun and the children, seated near the front of the crowd, stood and then resumed their places.

"Honey, I wonder if you'd come up here with me," Ryun continued to his wife. Then he addressed the crowd once more. "You know, since Anne and I were married in 1969 we've really been a team, and most everything I've participated in has involved the two of us. Anne was with me in Mexico City and Munich and was a much-needed partner in my running career. During these last twelve years, as we've been conducting running camps and speaking throughout the country, it really has been a joint effort. So I'd like her to be with me to help field and respond to your questions."

Anne, also wearing a running suit and smiling broadly, climbed the steps and joined her husband. She stood nearly a foot shorter than he but easily made up the difference with her buoyant enthusiasm.

Several hands shot into the air and one by one Ryun acknowledged them.

"What have you been doing for a living these last ten or fifteen years?"

"I majored in photojournalism at Kansas," answered Ryun, "and earned money when I was in school doing free-lance photography. After graduation I worked full time in that field for, let me see . . . probably about two years. Then for a time there was the professional track tour, which didn't mean much money but it helped us get by. And now I am a consultant for Nike, have occasional advertising contracts, and face a rather heavy speaking schedule."

"Tell us a little about pro track. How long did it last?"

"I ran with the ITA (International Track Association) for nearly the full duration, which was from 1973 to 1976."

"Were your performances good?" asked another. "I mean were you happy with your races as a professional?"

"Yes and no. I had very few what I would call quality races. The intensity of the schedule was very demanding. There was a heavy promotional side to my responsibilities that kept me quite tired from all the travel that went along with it. It was simply impossible to train adequately and race at optimum levels under the circumstances. But I have no regrets. I had a family to support and wanted to keep running. ITA made that possible and I'm grateful."

There was a slight pause and Ryun acknowledged another hand. "You were always portrayed as such a soft-spoken Mr. Nice Guy, full of humility and all. Was that a true picture?"

"As far as the nice guy part," responded Ryun sportively, "you'll have to ask my wife."

He smiled and laughter rippled through the crowd. "But seriously though," he continued, "I was very young and was thrust into the public spotlight so early in my life. I was extremely shy and reserved; it used to terrify me to be asked to speak, even to a handful of sixth graders. And now look at me . . ."—he gestured toward himself with his free hand—". . . here I am in front of you, relaxed and having a good time of it! Yet I did keep a lot inside during those years when I was receiving so much notoriety. The pressure of the public expectation was enormous."

"Anne," called out a woman runner, "what's it like being married to such a running celebrity?"

Anne laughed. "I'm his greatest fan," she said, then laughed again. "I used to like it, traveling all over the world for meets. But after a while the pace and demands of Jim's position and reputation did wear me down. There was very little time left just for us; the press found its way into every corner of our family. But now that our priorities are restructured, I love the opportunities we have to meet people and to share with them."

"Do you run too?" another woman asked.

"Yes," said Anne, "on and off. But it's not part of my makeup like it is for Jim. It *hurts!*"

Another wave of laughter swept through the crowd.

"Jim," shouted out a voice from the back. "You look lean and fit. Are you racing again?"

"I started running in some road races about five years ago and have really been enjoying it. The camaraderie is great! You can only stop running for so long. It gets in your blood."

"What's your best 10K time?"

"My recent best is 31:26; I never ran one back during my track days. But I don't always do that well. Today I think my time was 32-something, not much under 33 minutes. As you can see, I'm not much of a distance runner. I'd like to try a marathon some day, but I suppose I'm still a bit intimidated."

"Think you'll ever get back on the track?"

"Oh, I look forward to maybe getting into some low-key 5000-meter runs, just for fun. I love running and working out on the track and will probably keep doing some of that, along with road running, all my life. Without the pressure on me, I'm free to enjoy it all."

"How long did you hold the mile record?"

"Eight or nine years, something like that. Aren't these guys today something? Wow . . . what a time to be a miler!"

"Has anyone else ever held the record that long?"

"Oh, sure. Gunder Haegg in the '40s had it a long time. That was before Bannister's run. And then there was an incredible guy back in the 1800s by the name of Walter George who held it a really long time. That guy's feats were positively amazing. He has to rate as one of the greatest milers of all time, along with Elliott, of course."

"If you used to be so timid, how do you explain the change?"

"There are a lot of factors," Ryun began, then paused momentarily. "In so many respects I am a different person now than I was then. As most of you know, I am a Christian. That is certainly the biggest factor. As I have grown, the Lord has in so many ways remade me. And then the running camps have also helped boost my confidence, being around kids."

"Tell us something about the camps."

"We started them in 1973 and held three or four nearly every year until 1981. They have been difficult administratively, setting up week-long camps in different parts of the country, arranging for food, lodging, insurance, travel, facilities, and activities. It's completely nonprofit and Anne and I take care of all the business aspects ourselves. So it's quite taxing. But we really enjoy working with young runners. It's very rewarding and we hope to continue conducting them periodically, probably to a lesser degree than before."

"So many of the big-name runners have made so much money, in business and from other running spin-offs. Do you have any plans to go into business or TV and do something on the basis of your name?"

"Not really. We live very simply. Our family is our priority. We don't want to get so caught up in activities and money-making pursuits that the unity and harmony among the six of us breaks down. There are always offers, of course, but that just isn't the kind of life-style we want to get into. We pray about every incoming situation on the basis of how it will affect our children, our family life together, and what we feel the Lord wants us to do."

"Where are you living now?"

"After ten years in California, we've recently relocated back in Lawrence, Kansas. We have a home in the country where we feel very comfortable about our children growing up. As much as is possible with the responsibilities I have, we try to keep to a simple way of life."

"Yours was such an up-and-down career. Has it been difficult to adjust to life after running—you know, the aging athlete syndrome?"

"I used to think that running was everything, the only thing that could give me meaning. But I've discovered a lot more in life recently that has offered more fulfillment and joy than running ever did."

"Has your life since running been a letdown—no more honors and acclaim?"

"Quite the contrary! I couldn't be happier. My life these past twelve years has been more exciting than ever. I wouldn't trade the experiences I've had with the Lord for anything. And I truly mean that!"

"Jim," asked another, "how did you get started in running?"
There was a long silence as the crowd awaited his reply.

"I'd always wanted to be an athlete," Ryun began at length, "but as a young boy I possessed very little ability to go along with that desire. But the dream burned deep inside."

He paused again.

"In fact," he said, "I can remember one incident very clearly . . ."

CHAPTER 1

The Need to Be Someone

"James," I could still hear my grandmother calling. "James, it's time for dinner. And it's practically dark. Come on in now."

"Just a few more throws, Grandma," I answered. "I've almost got this guy struck out. Two more outs and I've won the game."

I couldn't have been more than eight or ten, and one of the highlights of a visit to my grandparents' home in Colorado Springs was standing tall on the mound and facing a barrage of imaginary hitters. I wound for the delivery and burned in another fastball.

"Strike three!" I called and scooped up the ball as it ricocheted back to where I stood. I pounded it into my mitt, eyed the rock-wall backstop intently, and prepared to fan still another powerless batter. If I could hit a large, white, strategically placed rock located waist-high in the five-foot retaining wall, it was a strike. If I missed, it was a ball.

For hours I stood there and practiced. I wanted so desperately to be a *real* pitcher some day, on a *real* team. Matter of fact, I just wanted to be on any team. If I couldn't be a pitcher, I'd play anywhere. If not baseball, any sport would do.

Just making the team! That was the dream.

The reality, however, was that at school tall and gangly Jim Ryun usually found himself standing around with three or four others, hands in his pockets, waiting nervously after everyone else had been chosen, no matter what game they were waiting to begin. I was awkward, slow, and uncoordinated. And just as athletics did not set me apart, neither did academics. I was just not particularly interested in school.

Yet something inside me wanted to be more. One day while walking alone across the playground I came across a small scrap of wood. I picked it up, etched my name on it, and then buried it in the sand. This was my small way of creating a tiny slice of fame and immortality—placing my name on a plaque where it couldn't be destroyed.

During my younger grades, when my parents were both working, I returned from school and spent several afternoon hours in the house by myself. My brother didn't get home till later, so I often passed the time watching the old black-and-white "Superman" show on television. My deep desire to set myself apart, to be someone special, drew me like a magnet to Clark Kent's daring exploits as the Man of Steel. I was at an impressionable age and wanted to be able to do the same things.

One day after the show was over, I stood up, turned off the set, and said to myself, "I'm going to do what he just did." But since I knew I couldn't go to some distant planet to gain supernatural powers, I thought, "I'll mix myself an incredible drink! I'll drink it just once and it will supply me with permanent energy to become a boy superman. I'll fly through the air. I'll save people. Bullets will bounce off me. I'll crash through walls and run faster than cars!"

Excitedly, I ran into the kitchen, grabbed the tallest drinking glass I could find in the cupboard, and headed toward the refrigerator with great anticipation. I opened the door, scanned the shelves for a moment, and then began gathering small portions of everything I could lay my hands on. In went a little dill pickle juice, some Coca Cola, a shot of mustard and ketchup, orange juice, some leftover chicken gravy, a little milk, iced tea, cider vinegar, Worchestershire sauce, and so on. My drink included some of *everything* in that refrigerator!

But still I wasn't quite satisfied. I hastily turned toward the other side of the kitchen where my mother kept her spices, and one by one I added a few shakes from a number of the containers—cayenne pepper to cloves—into my Superman drink. When I was satisfied, I stirred the whole thing vigorously and headed with it out onto the back porch.

Slowly I took a long swallow from the glass—miraculously, without throwing up—set the drink down, lifted my arms above my head as I'd seen Superman do so many times, and leaped into the air, fully expecting to soar into the blue over our back yard.

Unfortunately, nothing happened. "Well, I haven't had enough of my drink," I thought to myself. So I climbed back up the short two steps onto the landing and drank down the remainder of my concoction. Unbelievably, I was still not sick! I lifted my arms high above me once more, and out I jumped.

The distance this time did seem to be a foot or two longer than before, but it was clear that the progression toward full flight was not coming along rapidly enough to merit my continuing on. Besides, I wasn't about to drink another one of those drinks in order to become Superman.

I turned and walked rather dejectedly back into the house.

The reality of my actual self and my realistic abilities knocked my self-esteem lower with every passing year. So I turned to other ways of propping up my low image of myself. I taught myself to swear, took up smoking, and in sixth grade got into a fistfight in which I received a nasty bloody nose. As I continued trying to act the tough guy, I caused several teachers great distress and my poor attitude ultimately got me kicked out of school for a day.

I had always been taught that smoking was wrong. Still it made me feel tough, more like "a man." Near our home was a bushy, evergreen shrub. Deep in the middle of that bush I kept a plastic tackle box that contained assorted cigarettes, cigars, and matches. Every morning when I arose at 5:00 for my paper route, my first order of business was to procure my tackle box from its hideout, ride my bike down the street just out of sight of the house, at which point I would stop and light up. Naively oblivious to the easily recognizable traces of smoke odors, I continued in this habit for two years, always stashing the box in the shrub after each morning's route. It never crossed my mind that anyone would find out or that the box, only twenty feet from the house, could ever be discovered.

From such beginnings, the discrepancy between the values I had been taught and the life-style I was secretly adopting grew wider and wider. Before long I was frequenting the local bowling alley with friends from church to play the pinball machines. We became so skilled that we racked up free games that we then sold at discount rates to earn money for our cigarettes and junk food. Had my parents known I spent my free time in such a place, I would probably have been soundly thrashed, but I managed to keep my comings and goings secret.

While at the bowling alley we soon began to observe the regularity of a certain delivery truck, brimming with freshly baked pies, making its appointed rounds several days a week. It took us very little time to discover that the pie man left his truck unlocked while making his delivery through the bowling alley's rear entrance. It took us an equally short time to devise a daring scheme whereby one of us would act as a scout just inside the door, standing guard to give the rest of us the high sign when the coast was clear. Many a marvelous lunch we scooped out of those pie tins with our hands after we'd run to hide behind a church nearby.

Having mastered one escapade, it is always easier to advance still further. Before long I was stealing the corner drugstore blind, taking comics that I gave to my friends, candy, gum, and other small items. But although outwardly there had been such an erosion of my values, the entire time my conscience played havoc with me. Eventually I tried to retrieve as many of the comic books as possible, which I then returned to the drugstore under my jacket and stuffed back into the comic rack. Knowing, however, that my secret returns in no way made up for all I had taken, I resorted to an alternate action.

On several occasions I went into the store to buy a ten-cent candy bar, handed the druggist a dollar bill with all the confidence of a genuine big-time spender, said, "Keep the change!" and turned to leave the store before he could say a word.

Nearly all these activities were being carried out totally apart from my family. I was brought up in the rigidly strict Church of Christ, whose doctrine appeared to me at my age to be nothing more than a long list of prohibitions—no smoking, no drinking, no dancing, no movies, and even no music in any form. Never so much as a single note was ever heard within the hallowed halls of the church. In the stressing of this list of *don'ts,* there was never any focus on an individual with his own unique identity and worth.

This conservative church life spilled over into our home as well, and I found little in either place that provided me with much encouragement. The night I discovered my tackle box missing from the shrub in front of our home, I was terrified to sit down at the dinner table, absolutely certain that my father had made the fateful discovery. I did manage to find the courage to show up for supper, took my place with an unusual degree of caution, and waited.

But my father never said a word about it. Although I was fear-struck each time he opened his mouth, dinner passed uneventfully and I left the table, apparently reprieved from my doom.

The tackle box was never mentioned, and I never saw it again.

It was not that one day I suddenly decided to violently rebel against this legalism in which I had been raised, but as I approached junior high school my "secret" life diverged more and more from the standards I had been taught were right. Since my forays into the forbidden regions of sin had not, as I half expected, resulted in my instant annihilation by a bolt of lightning, I began to wonder about the whole notion of the wrathful God that had been drilled into me since birth. After all, I seemed to have gotten away with it without being struck by lightning.

Therefore, my smoking, fighting, and excursions to the bowling alley, as well as my later involvement in sports, offered welcome opportunities to get out from under that stifling and legalistic environment. They provided outlets that gave me a degree of peer approval, occasional success, and a sense of being "in" with the group.

Being an athlete had always been my goal. I'd played some church-league basketball and tried out for the junior high team, but I was cut. I'd played Little League baseball on our church's team. As I grew older and the baseline distance grew from thirty to forty-five feet, I was too weak to throw the ball from my third baseman's position to first base. It would always bounce en route. "Come on, Ryun," I could hear the coach yelling, "this isn't a bowling game! You're supposed to *throw* it, not roll it." I was ultimately cut from that team, too.

My athletic options were severely limited. There was no junior high football at that time and soccer hadn't yet become popular in this country. The high school track was located across a field from the elementary school I attended, and one day someone called my attention to the older runners working out there.

"They must be nuts," I said. "That doesn't look like much fun."

I went golfing and bowling with friends, but they weren't "in" sports at school. If I was ever to attain the prestige of wearing a letterman's sweater, I had to find something else.

What else was there left to try but track?

Thus I eventually found myself trying out for the Curtis Junior High School track team in the longest event they had to offer, the quarter mile. I'd already tried the fifty-yard dash the year before and not only was I too slow but I also pulled a muscle in the process. I'd tried the hurdles in seventh grade. I'd attempted the long jump with no success. I even gave the pole vault a try but knocked myself out when my long, flailing legs, the crossbar, and the pole somehow got entangled and sent me crashing to the ground.

It seemed there was no place an awkward 6'1" fifteen year old could fit in.

So there I was in the spring of 1962, a ninth grader, set to try my fortunes again. I walked to the starting line on the dirt track. The PE teacher in charge of track held a stopwatch in his hand and explained that the race would be one lap around, a quarter of a mile, and that the first two finishers would get to represent Curtis in this event at the upcoming track meet. Silently I stood listening, looking down at my long, spindly legs, towering above all the other boys standing there with me. At last the moment came. The coach said, "On your marks; get set . . ."

I bent my knees and crouched in readiness.

"Go!" he shouted, and we were off.

I dashed off toward the curve, my long legs eating up the ground. As I led the way around the dusty, uneven track, I thought, "Hey, this is great!" So I poured it on even more.

Down the backstretch we flew. By the halfway point something began to happen I hadn't anticipated—I was tired. My heart was pounding and my legs were getting heavier and heavier to lift. I had definitely started too fast.

Through the next curve I went, slowing down with each successive stride. Some of the others had caught me by now and were even starting to go by. I gave it a gallant try, but it was obvious my gasoline tank had run dry. I'd had my first experience of dying in the homestretch! A few moments later I had run 58.5, finished out of the money, didn't make the team, and stood alone on the track bending over with hands on my knees, gasping desperately for air.

Despondently, I slowly walked home that afternoon. I had almost convinced myself that running was something I might be able to do as well as some of my classmates. I guess I'd been wrong.

Yet throughout the following weeks and months, as I reflected on my brief track career that had ended in failure, I thought that maybe I hadn't done so bad after all. If I didn't get any better in some other sport, well . . . maybe I could go out for track and, who knows, with a little work possibly get my quarter-mile time down to 53 or 52 seconds.

So I gradually began to think of running as a possible sport to participate in. Sure, at that point I would still have preferred to be an all-American basketball or baseball player. But facts were facts. If I couldn't get the ball across the diamond, I clearly didn't have much future as a big-league pitcher. However slow, at least I *could* run.

Whether a goal of a 53- or 52-second 440 was realistic or not, as I approached my entry into high school as a sophomore, more and more I wondered if I couldn't someday become a respectable 440 runner. I wanted earnestly to make good, and a dogged inner drive and self-discipline began slowly to propel me toward that goal.

CHAPTER 2

The New Sophomore at East High

The dream of someday succeeding in athletics remained with me as
I prepared to enroll in high school as a sophomore. Though running
had entered my mind as a potential avenue into the world of letter-
men's jackets and popularity, it remained but a blurry possibility.
I knew next to nothing about the sport itself.

Nevertheless I found I did enjoy the sheer physical aspects of
running. There must have been subconscious motivations I was
unaware of operating in me, for that summer following ninth grade
I found myself on several occasions out on the street in front of our
home running back and forth. It was a hot summer and what possessed that scrawny Ryun kid to dash back and forth, up and down
the block, dripping with sweat, must have been a question on the
minds of most of our neighbors. I never stopped to ask myself why
I was out there either. It was simply something that felt good in a
physical sort of way and made me feel good about myself. It never
dawned on me to ask where it might lead. So up the block I sprinted,
stopped for a breather, and then back down to our house, up and
back . . . up and back.

In late August, on my first day at Wichita's East High, there was
an orientation assembly for incoming sophomores. Among other
things, we were briefed on the ten interscholastic sports offered and
invited to remain afterward to hear more about the two fall sports,
football and cross-country. I knew football was out, and although
I had not an inkling of what *cross-country* meant, I decided to stay
anyway. Actually, I had a vague notion that cross-country had
something to do with running—wasn't it some kind of fall track?
—so I remained to listen.

"Many of you boys," the short, enthusiastic man began, "may have done poorly in junior high sports. But don't be discouraged. Everyone grows at a different rate and some of you still have plenty of growing to do. Someday you'll be as big and strong as those fellows you competed against in eighth and ninth grade. A lot of you will never be built for football. There's no way you can change that. But if you're willing to work, we'd like you to come out for cross-country. We think you just might enjoy it."

The speaker, cross-country and track coach Bob Timmons, had sparked a glimmer of interest inside me. And since I had already decided to participate in track the following spring, what could I lose by starting a little early?

That same afternoon I reported to the gym totally ignorant of what I would discover. If I'd had any idea they would make me run two miles, I probably would have turned around and headed for home right then. My concept of a "distance run" was still one lap around the track.

The large initial group met briefly in the gym to suit up. I didn't know anyone yet and scarcely spoke a word. I stood in front of my locker, taking in all the sights, sounds, and smells so unique to a high school locker room—the stale aroma of sweat mingled with dirty socks and worn-out tennis shoes, the clanging of metal lockers, the reverberating echoes of constant yelling. I pulled on my trunks, tied my tennis shoes, and headed out. There were a lot of older runners, obviously veterans to the routine, and I just followed along, having no idea what would come next.

Once everyone was ready, we headed at a slow jog up a long gradual incline for a park about a mile away. When we arrived, everyone stopped and began limbering up and stretching. I was ready for a breather. That was the farthest I had ever run at one time in my life and I was glad the workout was over!

I tried to copy the exercises I saw the others doing but finally lay down on the grass. "That was nice," I thought to myself, "but I'm ready to get back to the gym and head home."

It was a warm summer's day; my daydreaming was interrupted by a sharp voice.

"Hey you, Ryun!"

I turned around and glanced up. Everyone else had begun to jog again and was a couple hundred yards away.

"Come on. We're gonna start the workout."

"Start the workout?" I said to myself. "He's got to be kidding! I thought that *was* the workout!"

I dragged myself to my feet and began to jog after the others. I never dreamed there were races *longer* than the 440. Before long it became obvious—to my great dismay—that the run to the park had only been the warm-up. Now followed the workout!

It was a killer—eight half-mile loops around the park. And those guys ran fast! I gave it a gallant try. I staggered in at the end of the third one, in last place, hands on my knees, gasping for air.

"Recovery time is up," someone shouted, "we're ready to start the next half-mile!"

"Go away!" I wanted to say. "Leave me alone. Let me rest. I already feel like I'm going to die!"

I sat out the next two, tried one more, and that was it for the day. I was exhausted. I lay there on the grass, not caring that someone said that might cause my legs to cramp up.

It was a good thing the mile back to the gym was downhill; otherwise I'd never have made it. It also seemed like the ride home from school lasted forever. By the time I got there I was sick to my stomach and couldn't eat a thing for dinner. Neither could I study. I just wanted to flop down on my bed and lay there forever!

The next morning when I sleepily crawled out of bed to deliver my papers, my legs were so stiff and sore I could hardly stand.

You would think with a start like that I'd have quit. But the next afternoon I was suiting up in the locker room again. Trying to run, now that I was sore, was even more painful. But I'd dreamed of being an athlete and here I was, on a team, surrounded by other athletes, in the sporting environment of a locker room. Therefore, though the seemingly marathon distances were new to me, I stuck with it. I had soon bought my first pair of Converse size 12 running shoes and continued to work out with the distance runners after school.

I was later to learn that Coach Timmons kept detailed records on all his runners. More than once in those first weeks my name kept popping up as "Ryan," and there were scarcely any notations entered by the name of this bony, new sophomore with the awkward, head-wobbling style.

After a few days of workouts, a time trial was scheduled—a

one-mile run. I ran my first mile in 5:38, finishing the final quarter-mile in 94 seconds, way back in fourteenth place.

Maybe the chess team, or ping-pong . . .

"Give it up, James," my parents would say.

"Ah, it's not that bad," I replied.

"Not that bad!" exclaimed my mother. "You hardly ate two bites at dinner because you didn't feel well, and you're always exhausted. How can you say it's not that bad?"

I shrugged and didn't reply. I knew they were just concerned for me.

"It's too hard on you," said my dad. "You've got to remember, James, that most of those other fellows are older. They've been doing it longer. Your body isn't accustomed to the level of work."

"But I enjoy it," I said finally.

My parents just looked at each other with a sigh as if to say, "Well, you know, these days you just can't tell kids anything."

They were right—the workouts were tough. Coach Timmons was one of the pioneers in prescribing hard work for young runners, and we ran anywhere from ten to fifteen miles a day, usually in intervals of some kind. I remember with great joy the first day I completed five miles without stopping. Even the coach noticed. It was usually all I could do just to keep pace with the rest of the group, usually from somewhere at the end of the pack.

Even though I had dabbled with short-distance running from time to time, running four, six, even ten miles at a time was utterly new to me. Therefore it took several weeks for the conditioning to begin to show, but gradually I did begin to improve.

At 3:00 each afternoon we gathered in the old gym, dressed to train, and went out for our run. The distances and intensity of the workouts steadily increased, as did my capacity to do them. When the season began, I was simply one obscure face in a crowd of twenty or thirty varsity and junior varsity runners. As the conditioning began to strengthen my legs and muscles and my heart and lungs, suddenly an incredible thing started to happen—I began to finish ahead of more and more of my teammates. We raced every week, and each time I was higher on the list and my times were faster and faster.

I could not explain what was going on; neither could anyone else. But the dramatic improvements continued throughout the fall.

Walking to class at East High.

By the time that first cross-country season was over, I was looking ahead to spring track with definite interest and anticipation.

However, I still had some reservations. My attitude toward running was something of a love/hate relationship. I loved the feeling of success, but how I hated the *pain!* So I did very little running during the winter and continued to keep my options open, wondering if something else might turn up in the spring. I'd won a set of weights with a friend for our finish in a 50-mile run/walk. I daydreamed about getting into competitive weight lifting. What better way to overcome my ninety-seven–pound weakling image? And I had done some golfing . . .

Yet in the back of my mind was the vision that maybe someday I could be a miler. It was probably this idea, an even more lofty dream than my earlier aspirations to run a fast 440, that prompted me that winter prior to my first track season to buy a cheap stopwatch in a downtown discount house. A few days later I took it with me to the high school track. I thought I'd try a mile on the track for time, just for fun, to see what I could do.

The day was cold and windy. I looked around to make sure no one was watching me, dragged my foot across the track to make myself a start and finish line in the soft dirt, shivered from the wind, and then stretched a couple of times just for good measure. All good runners seemed to stretch before they did anything, so I thought I should follow all the right procedures.

At last I walked up to my starting line, clutched the watch, and took off. I ran hard but had no understanding of how to pace myself for each lap. The wind whistled by my ears, but by now I was no longer cold. Two laps . . . three laps . . .

In the last lap I was tired—real tired.

"Why bother, man. This hurts," I said to myself. About a hundred yards from the finish line I quit, turned off the track, and walked home.

As spring approached, the track team began to assemble for daily workouts after school. The abilities that had begun to surface during cross-country were still there, but I was so quiet and unsure of myself that I hardly grasped any of the significance behind it. However, it was clear to the coaches and other runners that when the Lord put together this body of mine, He put within it what can only be viewed as a number of remarkable uniquenesses. Over the coming years my accomplishments on the track always struck me as events happening to someone else. Inside I was still just the *me* I had always been. But on the track, the runner Jim Ryun—he was someone else. I could almost stand back and observe myself, in as much disbelief as anyone over the remarkable achievements.

The first mile race of my sophomore track season was to be held in late March. Even though my previous best mile was 5:38, because of my improvements during cross-country I, a lowly sophomore, was to be pitted against junior and senior varsity runners. Not only that, to make matters worse, our opening meet set me against the previous year's state mile champion of all of Kansas. I felt like a fifth grader entered in the Olympics. I'd never run an official competitive mile in my life, and now I had to line up against the best the state had.

Possibly in sheer ignorance of how good my opponents actually

The beginning of a cross-country workout.

were, I wasn't overly intimidated, however. I just figured I'd get behind the others, follow their pace, and stay with them as long as I could.

That's exactly what I did once the race began. However, someone had forgotten to mention to me that the idea isn't to follow the leaders *all* the way to the finish line, which is exactly what I did, my eyes glued to the back of Harper's stride all the way to the tape.

Watching the replay of the race that night on the ten o'clock news sports report was exciting. I think for the first time it began to dawn on me that I possessed a little bit of talent. Possibly I'd discovered that athletic niche I'd been looking for. As I sat there in front of the TV, I made up my mind that state mile champion Charlie Harper wouldn't beat me next time.

The following week we faced one another again. I walked up to the starting line, the gun went off, and the race developed along exactly the same lines as the previous week. I fell into stride automatically behind Harper's pace-setting red jersey and numbly remained there as the laps clicked by—one, two, three. As he increased his speed for the final kick to the tape, I mechanically stepped up my own tempo as well. This time I wasn't going to stay behind him in a trance!

The morning after the race, every copy of the *Wichita Eagle* I tossed to the houses along my route carried my picture and name in headlines. I couldn't help feeling a certain pang of prideful embarrassment as I stopped every so often to reread the article:

Sophomore Jim Ryun of East overtook North's defending state champion Charles Harper in the last 50 yards and beat him to the finish line by two strides, setting a meet mile record of 4 minutes, 26.4 seconds. Ryun . . . stayed on the North star's heels throughout the race until he sprinted past him at the finish. [*Wichita Eagle*, March 30, 1963]

The following weeks proved significant ones. Coach Timmons had been understandably excited about my performance. I had no inkling of what was to come or what he was thinking. My biggest ambition at the time was to win at the state meet. That represented the ultimate.

He mentioned his wild thought to me that week. I scarcely can recall the incident. It took the more thoughtful setting of a bus trip home from Kansas City after the following week's meet for his words to sink in.

Every long bus ride has those moments, especially if you're traveling at night, when the mood somehow calms and everyone settles into their own quiet corner of thought. A couple guys might be quietly talking, someone else listening to his radio, maybe a card game is going on in the back of the bus, but the raucous, loud yelling and horsing around so common to a high school atheltic team has subsided for a few moments.

During one of these times, Coach Timmons called me to the front of the bumpy-riding yellow school bus where he made room for me on the seat beside him.

"Let's talk about goals," he began. "What do you think you can do a mile in?"

"This year?" I said. "Oh, I don't know, maybe—"

"Not this year," interrupted the coach. "I mean by the time you're a senior . . . ultimately."

I'd never really given it any thought.

"I guess maybe 4:10," I said.

Timmie paused and began gathering and shuffling his papers as

My first Kansas Relays mile, at fifteen (in early 1963), against other Kansas high schoolers, including Charles Harper from North High. The time was 4:21.3.

he always does before he has something important to say. "Jim," he began, "this is what I think."

He paused, then continued, "I've been keeping a chart of your performances."

He pulled out his clipboard and began to show me some numbers and lines drawn. Pointing down, he looked at me. "Do you see what I'm driving at, Jim?"

I stared at him without saying anything.

"I'm talking about the four-minute mile, Jim. No high school boy has ever run one. I think you can be the first, if you're willing to go after it and work for it. I'm convinced you can do it."

I looked at him incredulously. My running experience was severely limited; I'd never heard of Paavo Nurmi, Herb Elliott, and barely of Roger Bannister. I did know enough to realize that a four-minute mile was worlds away. My unspoken response was simply, "Coach, I think you're crazy!"

Nevertheless, Timmie had a vision without which I would have withered along the way. I'd have probably been a fairly successful high school runner. He planted within me the vision of even greater things, kept pressing me toward it, and didn't let me give up on myself.

Recalling the incident later, Timmons said, "As I look back on it, I am sure Jim did not comprehend the significance of our conversation at all."

It was just one of those life-altering moments that you look back on in later years. At the time, as he said, I had no idea what a four-minute mile signified. I had no notion of the flow of the history of mile running, that it had taken the best runners in the world nearly a century to break four minutes. I was only fifteen years old, basically still a child. Yet while I may have thought it absurd, in my ignorance, nothing about it inherently intimidated me. It could be likened to someone who knows virtually nothing about baseball, hearing that a .400 batting average is considered very, very good, saying, "Oh, okay. I think I'll play in the major leagues and bat .400." He has no idea what he's saying and no conception of the difficulty involved.

But Timmons was not to be dismayed. He was certain of my ability, even if I wasn't myself. He had already tutored several very successful milers and believed in his coaching system. He set out immediately to get me thinking like a four-minute miler and picturing myself competing with the best in the country. As difficult as it was to make the adjustment to consider myself a champion, a front-runner, as a "good" athlete, I did my best to trust in the coach's judgment and to believe his words.

"You'll have to get used to people making fun of you and even ridiculing your efforts," he warned. "For a boy with your uncertainty and reticent personality, that may be as hard as the workouts themselves. You're trying to do something nobody your age has ever tried before. I admit I don't know how my timetable will work out. We may have to adjust things as we go along. Neither of us will know until we get there. And that's the tough part, Jim. You'll be out there all by yourself. You're going to leave high school competition far behind."

Though I was initially dumbfounded by his prediction, it did in fact prove not only to be accurate but to set me on target for what would be the essence of my life for some time to come.

CHAPTER 3

In Pursuit of Four Minutes

Coach Timmons was as much philosopher as coach. Though at the time he held but a high school position, he was recognized as one of the best, centering his coaching theories around thorough planning, determined sacrifice, and hard work—all given direction and purpose through the use of specific goals for each runner. The very backbone of his program was rooted in goals. Very much still a novice myself, I relied on Coach Timmons in large measure to set me on course toward what he felt were reasonable goals, for he clearly had loftier visions for me at this point than I did. But I was willing to go along.

There were many races that year. As the times continued to drop, more than once Timmie's eyes popped when he looked down at his stopwatch, and he began to look toward stiffer and stiffer competition for me to face. By the end of the year I had run 4:08 as a sixteen year old and Timmie first made public the four-minute goal. What had originally been an almost casual approach to running was changing for me. Timmie crystallized the objective and I began to desire it with a far greater intensity than before—the hunger to accomplish what no one else had ever done.

My devotion to that goal became single-minded, my sole purpose for living. Gradually the success coming my way forced many of my youthful uncertainties and frustrations into the background. Running offered an escape from the self-doubts. It was a chance to succeed, it gave me the identity I had longed for, and thus I threw myself into it with enthusiasm and dedication.

Though I had few deep, personal religious convictions at this point, I still remained tied to the church framework I grew up in. There was an enigmatic sort of security there because the church environment was all I had known. I remained unsure of myself in most areas of life except running; I was a very unassertive young teenager, hesitant to voice my growing doubts. Thus there was a paradoxical relationship between my budding independence and my narrow church and home background. Part of me wanted to flex my wings and break free, while another part of me felt obligated to gain the church's sanction in order to make what I was doing acceptable. I partially resolved this dilemma by going to my minister to ask if it was proper to pursue the lofty ambitions Coach Timmons was placing before me.

"I've come to you for some guidance about my running," I said. "It's impossible to maintain the same commitment to church as before—Sunday mornings, Sunday evenings, Wednesday nights— when training takes such a drain and I often don't feel well. I feel I'm expected to be here whenever the church doors are open, yet I have some high goals and want to be a success in running too."

I doubt I'd have altered my plans whatever he said, but in an extraordinary moment of liberality his response was "If you don't set your goals high, you'll never reach them. If you're going to go into this thing, a Christian ought to do his very best."

His words were reassuring. Yet it's difficult for most people to comprehend the level of sacrifice involved in attaining something like being the best in your particular field. It means you basically do nothing else. You eat, breathe, and sleep your goal. At this point I was eager to jump headlong into it; my life previously had been so drab and running offered purpose. I was young, only sixteen. I was hardly mature enough to determine what impact these goals— especially if I attained them—would have on my later life. My duties at sixteen were simple, unconfusing, and one-dimensional. Running became my life, my consuming passion. Timmie served as my mentor, my folks provided for my needs, and all I had to focus my attention on was getting better.

As my junior year opened and with it another cross-country season, the daily workouts increased in intensity. Still there were races every week, but I hardly rested up for them because Timmie was eyeing the following spring track season. So we worked nearly every day, most weeks containing at least one long run of 15 to 20 miles as well as frequent interval work. By midwinter Coach Timmons had increased my mileage to 110 miles a week—sixteen miles a day. Most of it was covered alone and often under grim conditions. Kansas winters can be harsh—snowdrifts, fierce biting winds,

During a speed-workout on the track, Bob Timmons, my high school coach, in foreground.

gusty rain, muddy roads. Sometimes I would carry a portable radio to while away the monotony of the long miles. Not that I didn't enjoy it most of the time. But it was a demanding regimen for one so young.

One day I walked into the coach's office, very dejected, sick of running in the dark with rain pounding in my face, slushing through the snow watching the perspiration freeze in the wrinkles of my sweats, day after day. I was beginning to wonder if it was worth it. I expressed my discouragement to the coach, who listened very patiently from behind his desk.

"Sometimes I just don't think I can take it anymore, coach," I said. "It gets so boring. I get tired of it."

"There's no other way to reach the top, Jim. It takes hard work."

"But the rain, the snow! It was ten degrees outside this morning. Ten degrees! And the wind was blowing besides!"

Timmie listened to me spout off all my frustrations. When I had finished he sat there silently for some time. Finally he said, "Look, Jim, if this goal of a four-minute mile isn't worth enough to get out and work for day after day, forget it. Nobody's going to browbeat you into achieving something you don't want to do yourself. I'm not going to stand over you with a whip. But I don't want you to come back to me after it's all over and tell me you would have made it if I had made you work harder."

Slowly I rose from my chair and left his office.

Needless to say, I continued.

Keeping up such a schedule was very demanding. I had very little social life, was sick many evenings, and usually didn't get home until 6:30 or 7:00. This allowed me time only to eat a warmed-up meal, do a little homework, and then go to bed to ready myself for a repeat of the grueling routine the next morning.

As spring neared and with it the outdoor season of my junior year, my afternoon workouts again took more the form of intervals. I did many 440 repeats. I recall one early-season workout of forty 440's in an average pace of 69 seconds, each with about a 90-second rest between them. It was a killer! And so monotonous. The goal was everything. The magic number was permanently imprinted in my brain—4:00.

Because I was on a high school track "team" there were numerous meets to be run, but none of these were looked upon as important. It was not until May, after the high school season was past, that Timmie felt ready to at last send me out against the best milers in the United States.

The first big invitational race came at the California Relays in Modesto. I'd just turned seventeen and was going to face three greats who had all run 3:56 or better—Dyrol Burleson, Tom O'-Hara, and Cary Weisiger. There were some who were not pleased to find me—a mere schoolboy—in the race at all. Coach Timmons approached an official prior to the competition to ask whether 1500-meter times would be given. He was informed that they would be for the better runners, "but not for Ruin or Runyon or however you pronounce it." A statement was made by Mike Igloi, a premier distance coach recognized throughout the world, expressing dissatisfaction that "the meet management has invited an untried kindergartner to compete in the mile."

To an extent, these criticisms were justified. With a best time of 4:06, I was green and untried. But it just heightened my determina-

My parents greeting me at the airport after one of many trips.

tion to do well, as did word we received prior to the race that Gerry Lindgren had beaten my high school record with a 4:06 mile in the Washington State Meet.

Naturally I was very nervous before the race. As had become my custom, I sought out a quiet, secluded spot before the race during my warm-up and said the simple prayer, "God, please help me and my competitors to do our best and to be able to live with the results." (This bit of ceremony became less and less significant, however, as I grew more successful.)

I'd never experienced such heady competition. I settled in at the back of the pack as the race got underway and suppose I was unnoticed for the first very slow lap of 63 seconds. I remained last at the halfway point in 2:05, but we were all closely bunched. I hung on as a couple others fell back and was sixth at the 1320 in 3:06. The pace increased as the leaders jockeyed for position and Burleson and O'Hara widened their lead on the rest of us. As they fought it out for first place, I was desperately sprinting into the last curve and down the final straightaway. I've been told later that the crowd, knowing I was the schoolboy dark horse, began to shout and cheer for me, not believing I could still be with such renowned milers. I sprinted for all I was worth and beat Weisiger in a dead heat for third in an incredible 4:01.7.

1. Dyrol Burleson   4:00.2
2. Tom O'Hara   4:00.3
3. Jim Ryun   4:01.7
4. Cary Weisiger   4:01.7
5. John Camien   4:02.2
6. Bob Seaman   4:04.2
7. Peter Keeling   4:14.5
8. Richard Green   4:17.7

The following week another major race was scheduled at the Compton Invitational in Los Angeles. Timmie had advised me to go right out rather than holding back as I had done the previous week. Therefore I started out near the front of the pack in what was a much faster early pace. Unfortunately, in the second lap I was bumped as we jostled in the midst of the dense crowd.

Someone with good balance would probably have recovered easily, but as an infant I had suffered a very high fever that permanently damaged the nerves in my inner ear. It left me with a 50 percent hearing loss as well as occasional dizziness and equilibrium problems. Right in the middle of the race I was suddenly very much off balance. When I'm running it's similar to being on stilts, and the slightest jarring of my stride can send me down in a heap the next moment. As soon as Timmie learned of this, he began drilling into me the words "If ever you fall in a race, jump up and get back into the competition quickly." Fortunately on this occasion I somehow managed to remain on my feet as I awkwardly stumbled across the curb and into the infield, nearly falling on my face. Recovering myself I kept moving, and when all the other runners had gone by I hastened back onto the track and took off after them.

I'd lost my rhythm and concentration, not to mention valuable energy. Therefore I contented myself with holding onto the rear of the pack and made no attempt to get back in touch with the leaders. I was shocked with how fast I passed the halfway point—2:01.5. I remained where I was through the third and halfway into the last lap. But then down the homestretch everyone sprinted and ran away from me. I was able to catch no one and finished next to last.

Very disheartened, I thought I had run poorly. Then the announcer came over the public address system after a few moments, saying that for the first time in history, eight men in one race had just broken the four-minute mile.

"Did I finish eighth or ninth?" I wondered. I couldn't remember and was far too fatigued to think clearly. I had to wait in suspense for the official announcement.

Finally it came, ". . . in eighth place, Jim Ryun in a time of three minutes, fifty-nine seconds flat."

1. Dyrol Burleson 3:57.4
2. Tom O'Hara 3:57.6
3. Archie San Romani, Jr. 3:57.6
4. Morgan Groth 3:57.9
5. Jim Grelle 3:58.5
6. Bob Day 3:58.9
7. Cary Weisiger 3:58.9
8. Jim Ryun 3:59.0
9. Bob Delaney no time

Although Timmie's original goal had been reached, there was no time to relax. This was 1964, an Olympic year, and immediately Timmie began talking about the Olympic Trials. Such a dream would have seemed unreachable only a week earlier. Now, despite the fact that I was only the eighth or tenth best miler in the country and only the top three would make the team for Tokyo, I was only a second or two away from Burleson and O'Hara. Timmie thought I could do it. I wasn't so sure.

Up to this point my times had attracted mostly localized interest with merely scattered bits of wider attention. Suddenly, having run four minutes as a high school junior just a month beyond my seventeenth birthday, there began to be instant national recognition. In another three months *Sports Illustrated* would, incredibly, choose me for their front cover, and from that moment on such notoriety followed me wherever I went. Hardly a day went by when some Kansas paper or magazine did not run some kind of story on "the amazing kid from Wichita." I began to be asked for interviews (and even to see things in print I'd had no prior knowledge of) from all manner of magazines—from *Time, Look, L'Equipe* and the *London Times* to *Teenage Christian, Junior Scholastic, Coronet,* and *Amateur Athlete* to dozens of Sunday newspaper supplements. Letters and phone calls began to pour in, and in one sense my life ceased to be my own. All

Working with Coach Timmons on his farm during the summer of 1964.

the while, down inside a little voice kept saying, "Is this really happening to me? This can't be *me* who's done these things these people are writing about."

The Olympic Trial finals were three months away in Los Angeles. Only the top three would make the trip to Tokyo representing the United States in the 1500. During those summer months I lived with Coach Timmons, his wife Pat, and their four children at a farm outside Lawrence. He trained me that summer, between farm chores, with great intensity. I ran miles and miles of solitary country roads and every afternoon we went to the University of Kansas stadium to do intensive interval and speed work on the track. Something about the farm atmosphere had always been special to me ever since my earliest recollection of my uncle's farm where I helped with the cows and loved to roam the countryside and fish in a nearby lake. I especially enjoyed that summer of 1964 with the Timmonses, cleaning out the barn, mowing weeds, fighting a cantankerous tractor. It was a pleasant respite from the track and road work.

Yet despite my track success, I was personally still such a babe in the woods, so raw and so green. One evening when I was babysitting for the Timmons's kids, they asked me if I'd like to play a great game called "Fifty-Two Card Pick Up." Naturally, cards in any form had been strictly forbidden in our home as I'd grown up, and I was as innocent as the day I was born of being made the butt of an impending joke.

"Sure," I said.

Moments later, though I was the oldest of the five present, I was down on my hands and knees retrieving the cards, to the wildly inexpressible delight of the youngsters who had this tall, shy runner completely buffaloed.

Just weeks before, staying in a hotel for a race with Timmie, I went into the bathroom to take a shower. When I was through, it was Timmie's turn. He walked into the bathroom and then hollered out at me.

"Hey, what's going on here? The floor's all wet!"

I walked in. He was right; the place was flooded.

Then he beckoned toward the shower. "Don't you know you're supposed to put the shower curtain *inside* so the water won't run all over the place?"

I shrugged. How was I to know? We had no showers in our home. I just hadn't been aware enough to even wonder what happened to the water. It wasn't so much that I was a country bumpkin. I was just unbelievably naive and oblivious to so much going on around me.

Timmie and I spent more time together that summer than ever before. It was an intense time. He talked straight to me. He was convinced I could beat one of the three—Burleson, Grelle, or O'Hara. At first I was hardly convinced. I'd been beaten by them—and many others—so frequently up till then. But as the work intensified and his pep-talk drills worked their way into my mind, I suppose I became conditioned to believe it myself. When it took pressure, he would apply it. As time went on, I saw what the hard work would do. Then I began to understand what Timmie was trying to accomplish.

But it was tough!

There was no racing that summer. We were pointing for one race and one race only. I worked by myself, against the clock, against the hot Kansas sun, and even at times against Timmie himself. The closer the Trials came, the more we both began to sense that I was ready.

The day finally came on September 13, 1964. The *Sports Illustrated* issue with my picture on the cover had just been released and I hoped I wouldn't suffer a jinx from it. Excitement ran high. The

Between intervals at the track, Coach Timmons applied the pressure I needed to get me ready for the Olympic trials, Bill Dotson listens in.

media had given the race much coverage and out of the six 1500-meter finalists, any of us could make the team. The early pace was slow and even with only a lap to go all six were bunched up within four yards of one another. After all this preparation, it was going to be a 300-yard dash rather than a 1500-meter run!

Still no one made a move.

Suddenly the pace quickened and an all-out sprint for the tape was underway. I had been running on the outside, well into the second lane and took off with the rest. I had been in sixth, then moved up as one of the contestants faded. Coming out of the final curve, I ran wide in the third lane. There seemed little hope now. All the others in contention had outsprinted me previously. I was conscious of the option of merely finishing or of going for it. There was a pause in my brain. Even as I ran, in a split second of time, everything went into suspension while I considered that last hundred yards.

As we sprinted madly for the finish, Burleson and O'Hara led the way, I moved up on the outside, and Jim Grelle lunged forward toward the tape.

Then the thought came, "You've worked too long and hard to quit now." Suddenly the slow-motion pause ended and I took off with something extra. Whereas before they had been pulling away, now I was the one moving up on the outside. I moved into fourth place.

Burleson and O'Hara had opened up a slight gap. Jim Grelle led me by a couple of feet on the inside. The finish was approaching so quickly; it seemed an impossible margin to overcome. The stands were in a frenzy. I could see Grelle alongside and knew that this former Olympian who at this point had run more four-minute miles than anyone other than Herb Elliott was working every bit as hard as I was.

We crossed the finish—I in a dead sprint, Grelle lunging toward the tape, Burleson straining, O'Hara smiling. I wasn't sure who had

With both my coaches, Bob Timmons and J. D. Edmiston, in the stands following my third-place
finish.

won the coveted third position. Grelle lay motionless on the track
where he had fallen after his desperation dive, and I walked slowly
around the curve trying to recover.

When the results were announced, all four of us had finished
within .7 of a second of each other. The judge had concluded that I
had nosed out Jim Grelle in the photo finish by only a few short
inches.

I was an Olympian!

1. Dyrol Burleson   3:41.2
2. Tom O'Hara   3:41.5
3. Jim Ryun   3:41.9
4. Jim Grelle   3:41.9
5. Archie San Romani, Jr.   3:43.0
6. Bob Day   3:46.1

Accompanying Dyrol Burleson and Tom O'Hara to our places as part of the American Olympic Team in Tokyo.

CHAPTER 4

Climb to the Summit

What a distance I had come! I'd been running track a mere eighteen months. Suddenly the ugly duckling of Wichita, Kansas was on his way to the Olympic Games.

Naturally I was exultant. It was a time of great personal triumph. At this point in my life I hardly stopped to consider the long-term implications. I was not introspective about what was happening to me but content to be carried along on its crest.

Tokyo presented me with my first taste of failure in a long time. I felt healthy and had several excellent workouts after arriving in Japan. Then a virus hit me, as well as many others on the American team. After managing to get through my first 1500-meter heat, I was completely drained and finished dead last in the semifinal. I was extremely depressed and could hardly wait to get home, away from the Olympics, and on with school.

This was my senior year at East High and I raced through it—both during cross-country and track seasons—with a great deal more confidence than I had previously had. Coach Timmons had left Wichita to go to the University of Kansas, where he was an assistant coach for one year and would then became the head coach. My coach for the year was J. D. Edmiston, with whom I immediately developed a good relationship. By the summer of 1965, even the stiff national competitions did not frighten me to quite the same extent they had. There continued one factor, however, that remained a major and terrifying unknown. That was the spectre of three-time gold medalist and world-record holder Peter Snell from New Zealand. Rumors were flying that he would be touring the United States and would be entered in several races. The mere mention of his name was sufficient to send chills up the spine of any distance runner in the world.

A new factor I had to contend with was the press. No longer was I an upstart youngster. Wherever I went I was besieged by reporters, frustrated by my simple yes and no answers that struck them as mock humility on my part. They expected great outspoken confidence that it was just not in my nature to give. Though I was certainly growing more self-assured when stepping onto a track, down inside I remained timid and shy. My confidence was building, but the shell surrounding it still remained. I had not been trained in the graces of conversing with anyone, and I had no idea how to deal with reporters.

Our workouts were geared to prepare me to face Peter Snell and Jim Grelle in a race during the first week of June. My race plan was to stay with Snell all the way and move with him once he started his drive in the last 220. It would have seemed an easy strategy had we been talking about anyone other than the most dominant force in middle-distance running for four years. He had annihilated every major mile field he had ever faced.

I was very nervous as I glanced over at Snell on the starting line, awed by the company I was in. The pace of the race was quick and I remained toward the back of the pack with Grelle and Snell all the way. Even though I prepared myself mentally for it, when Snell made his powerful burst with half a lap to go, I was simply amazed. In an instant he was six yards in front and as hard as I sprinted I could not hope to make up the distance. I finished third.

I was pleased with my time. Though I had been close, I could still not help but consider Snell a hero. Who was I, at eighteen, to be compared with the Olympic champion and world-record holder?

Flying back to Kansas after the loss to Snell, I looked at things in a much different light. I suppose few people could have realized how greatly I'd begun to mature as a result of that race. It could well have been the first time I allowed myself to think of beating Peter Snell as but a stepping-stone toward the pinnacle of achievement. My photographer friend Rich Clarkson asked on the plane, "Is your ultimate goal to be the world's greatest miler?"

As I stared out the window of the jet, through all the doubts and fears of growing up, a portion of my dawning maturity as a runner came forth as I answered him simply, "Yes, I suppose it is."

Top to bottom: 1. Nervously eying the great Peter Snell at the starting line before racing against him for the first time. 2. At the finish, driving hard, I could not hope to make up the distance Snell and Grelle had suddenly opened up on me. 3. At the starting line for my second meeting against Snell I felt more confident. This time I had a plan. 4. This time the finish was different; our strategy had worked perfectly.

Another showdown was scheduled in three weeks in San Diego and we planned to reverse the outcome. We plotted out the race and realized that if I'd have moved first, Snell would have been forced to run wide and catch me. It was an important bit of strategy that formed a basis for the upcoming race.

We worked hard for three weeks and then returned to the west coast. There were almost daily happenings in the world of mile running that intensified interest in the upcoming duel. Michel Jazy had recently lowered Snell's world mile record to 3:53.6. And just a week later Jim Grelle had beaten Snell in Vancouver with a new American record of 3:55.4. Publicity and interest in the mile ran at a feverish pitch and prior to the San Diego race Snell was predicting he'd set a new world mark.

The day of the race I rested in our hotel room. JD went down to the press conference where Snell was fielding questions. There was talk of Jazy's record run a couple weeks earlier and a wondering if this signaled the end of Snell's era of dominance. Snell reaffirmed that tonight's race could well produce another record run and said he felt ready for a good one.

"What about Ryun?" someone asked.

"I doubt he'll be a serious factor in the race," answered Snell quickly, reflecting the view prevalent then in New Zealand and Australia that teenagers should not be developed so rapidly.

As soon as JD returned to tell me of Snell's comment, a little extra fuel was added to the fire already burning deep within. All day we reviewed our tactics. I could not again allow the others to gain the jump on me. If anyone was going to have to run wide around the curve, I had to make sure it wasn't me. Moving soon would give me the initiative. But if I went with a full 300 yards to go, we felt I might not be able to sustain it. So our strategy boiled down to this: I would move up into position with a lap and a half to go. Then, just before the last backstretch I would move quickly into the lead. I would not try to sprint. I would simply get into the lead and then back off slightly and wait for Snell's move. When he tried to pass me, I would sprint with everything I had to force him to run around me and do the catching up.

Again I walked to the starting line against a field of the best milers the world had to offer. As always, Snell appeared confident. But I had a plan and was determined to give it everything I had.

The starter called us to our marks.

I dug my spikes into the hard asphalt track, aware that the huge crowd had grown completely silent. "Set!" he yelled and I bent down in readiness.

The gun cracked and we were off.

I was in last place for the first lap and next to last at halfway in a reasonable time of 2:00. We were all bunched together with Snell and Grelle just in front of me. Everyone was waiting, runners and spectators alike. The race was like a gathering cloud from which anything might erupt at any time.

Suddenly without warning the Czech Joseph Odlozil burst out of fourth place into a five-yard lead, and the crowd came alive with a roar of excitement. The field strung out quickly and I moved into third behind Grelle, with Snell right on my shoulders. We went into the final quarter and I knew that once I made my move I would have to keep going because Snell would be right behind me.

Now was the time for me to begin my move, before we reached the backstretch. I swung a little wide to avoid Grelle and gathered myself for a burst. Twenty yards from the end of the curve I spurted. I quickly caught the fading Odlozil, running hard but not quite all out, knowing I still had enough left for a good finishing sprint.

A great roar went up from the crowd. All at once I was in front and it scared me to death! You plan things, of course, but to have them go just like clockwork was another thing.

The spectators became noticeably partisan, cheering for the young American to stay ahead of the Olympic champion, for David to beat Goliath, the slim boy so vastly the underdog against the muscular and mature athlete. People were on their feet and the sound was deafening.

Down the backstretch I tried to pick it up while still not moving full out. Into the last turn I was conscious of Grelle moving alongside to my right. What a competitor he was! At that point I didn't know if I could do it or not. Snell was right on Grelle's shoulder, running wide in the second lane.

The plan had worked to perfection.

I came out of the final curve accelerating with a determination to give it every ounce I had. I was in perfect position and from there on it was sheer driving, all three of us nearly abreast. Grelle began to fade slightly, but Snell was coming in, the man whose finishing kick was the most feared in the world. He was so close I could see him to my right. My legs were heavy but I did not let up. If there was any reserve to dig into, now was the time.

After what seemed an eternity, I felt the tape across my chest. The three of us had finished within .2 of a second of each other. I had set a new American record of 3:55.3, and Snell threw his arm around my shoulder and congratulated me warmly.

1.	Jim Ryun	3:55.3
2.	Peter Snell	3:55.4
3.	Jim Grelle	3:55.5
4.	Josef Odlozil	3:57.7
5.	Cary Weisiger	4:04.9
6.	Harry McCalla	4:05.7
7.	Dave Farley	4:12.5
8.	John Garrison	4:22.3

That fall I planned to enter the University of Kansas at Lawrence. During the remainder of the summer I ran with the U.S. team in Europe. The means employed by the Russians to make sure their track-and-field team beat us at Kiev were most ingenious. Everything went smoothly enough until we reached Moscow. But there —despite the fact that this U.S./U.S.S.R. meet was one of the biggest sporting events in the Soviet Union all year and had been planned in minute detail for months—suddenly all sorts of things began to happen: visas and passports not in order, lost hotel reservations, missed planes, no communication. They sat us down for our first meal in one of Moscow's leading hotels before flying us on to Kiev. Not only was the meal terrible but we had to remain in the restaurant six hours. Some miscue about the plane, they said.

When we finally boarded the shuttle flight to Kiev, it was an ancient model DC-3. As we sat down on the rope-netting seats looking upward toward the front of the plane at what seemed a forty-five–degree angle, we were told to gather together such items as fountain pens and place them in small plastic bags we had been given. The reason: The plane was not pressurized and such things could burst after we were airborne. Unfortunately, there was no help for our ears; it was an extremely painful flight.

Arriving in Kiev, we were told there was no space for us at the hotel. The reservations were not in order. Gradually their objective of wearing down our resistance with the fatigue of travel was succeeding. It took many hours for our accommodations to be readied.

Once in the drab room, which I had to myself, I was so spooked by the whole series of events and jittery every time I saw an armed army guard that I barricaded myself in with a chair propped under the doorknob. I was taking no chances!

I wrote my folks a postcard that said, "We finally made it to Kiev after twenty-one hours of confusion and two hours sleep."

At six o'clock the following morning suddenly blaring over my room's radio was a harsh stream of something in Russian. I was jolted out of an uneasy sleep—the previous day's events had kept us up until after midnight the night before—and rushed to turn the crazy thing off.

But it was permanently on! The volume could be adjusted, but even cranking the dial to the lowest position did not reduce the crackling jibberish to the point where any further sleep was realistically possible.

I'd had enough!

I examined the cord hoping to unplug the device, but it was wired all the way through the wall. It could not be turned off, turned down, unplugged, or the station changed. With a mighty heave I yanked the cord from the wall. The sound stopped immediately. I then very carefully stuck the mangled end back through the hole in the plaster, hoping I would not be discovered, and flopped back down on my bed in a vain hope of getting a bit more rest.

Our first breakfast capped it off. At last we hoped maybe we'd get something our systems were used to. Surely, we thought, they understood an athlete's need for care before competition. But alas, what should greet us on our plates that morning but cow's tongue.

I'm really not that finicky an eater and can tolerate most things. But in the morning? You really must be kidding!

By the time of the meet many of us had diarrhea.

Needless to say, in the combined men's and women's competition, the Russians beat us—by one point.

Then, miraculously, suddenly our fortunes seemed to change. The food we were served for the rest of our time in Russia was quite good and familiar. There were no more foul-ups, and our plane out of the country was a modern jet *with* cabin pressurization.

In one of the most well-known quotes I ever made, when several months later I was asked, "Doesn't it bother you that you're missing so many of the pleasures of the average American teenager?" I replied, "Not at all. How many of them have ever been to Kiev?"

At the University of Kansas, my major was photo journalism.

In conjunction with my photographic studies,
I worked part-time for the *Topeka Capital-Journal,*
shooting sporting events—in this case, a Kansas basketball game—to make what extra
money I could.

It sounded good in the press. But I'm not sure I'd ever want to go back!

That fall after entering the University of Kansas I participated with the cross-country team and prepared for my first major indoor racing season. My daily routine changed drastically now that I was in college, away from home, and living a dormitory life. I got up about 5:15 for my morning workout through the streets of Lawrence in order to be through with breakfast in time for classes that often began at 7:30. In the evenings I often had to slip away to an unused classroom someplace to study because of the heavy flow of visitors and phone calls constantly coming my way.

I began a regimen that year as a freshman that would become my pattern for quite some time, essentially competing in three separate sports—cross-country, indoor track, and outdoor track. Each brought with it a new set of demands and during any given school year I ran between thirty and fifty races. Now that I was a public figure, the spectators didn't want me to let them down.

I recall one particularly interesting tactical indoor race, the Baxter Mile in Madison Square Garden. Jim Grelle and I both wanted only one thing, to beat one another. We were practically oblivious to the other competitors and unconcerned with the time. As it shaped up, the race just about got away from us. Notre Dame's Ed Dean, apparently with designs of his own, took off and opened up a good lead. As far into the race as the 1320, Dean still led by 40 yards. Grelle and I were asleep back in third and fourth place and the fans were incredulous; they thought Dean had stolen the race from the favorites. On the ninth lap of the eleven-lap race, I accelerated and turned it on after Dean. I guess I caught Grelle unexpectedly off guard; he sprinted too but I'd opened 5 quick yards on him. I steadily whittled Dean's lead down with a final quarter of 55 seconds, and Grelle slowly ate away at my 5-yard advantage. We caught the fading Dean about 200 yards from the finish and a dead-heat sprint was on. Grelle made it all back but about two feet and we were both timed in 4:02.2.

Yet after that highly competitive and exciting race, when the time was announced it brought with it a cascade of boos. In fact, the crowd was so upset they tossed popcorn from the balcony. I was confused, unable to understand why the crowd of 15,000 hadn't grasped the race strategy as it had unfolded.

This was one of my first tastes of the unquenchable public

Jim Grelle and I caught a surprising Ed Dean of Notre Dame just a lap from the finish in the 1966 Baxter Mile at Madison Square Garden.

At the finish I had held Jim off by, once again, the slimmest of margins.

Racing as a KU freshman, at National AAU championships in New York City.

expectation. It grew at the university as well, often from perfect
strangers. I was awakened in the middle of the night more than once
by phone calls, and reporters would call at all hours. Every day it
was something different—someone wanted a copy of my training
schedule, to take a picture, to shake my hand. I tried to be sympathetic, but it was not always easy.

Strange as it seemed to admit to myself, I'd become a celebrity,
a face in the news, a name in the headlines. It mushroomed to the
point where there were daily and weekly columns and articles all
over the country poking into the corners of the private life of the
soft-spoken runner from the Midwest. I became highly scrutinized.
In high school all I had to do was run. Although that was basically
what I wanted to do now, I couldn't avoid the increasing host of

additional concerns. It was not unusual for someone to be taking my picture while I was walking down a corridor or even right in the middle of a class or a study session. One magazine photographer followed me around campus for two days. After observing this, one of my instructors asked me, "Why is he taking your picture? Are you the typical college freshman or something?"

I looked at the photographer, gave a half shrug, and said, "What should I say?"

One of the highlights of the 1966 outdoor season came at the Coliseum Relays in Los Angeles where I was entered in the two-mile—as the slowest of all the competitors. The class of the field was clearly Kip Keino and it was the first time I had faced him.

Keino immediately took the lead, wearing his famous orange baseball cap that he always ceremoniously took off and flung away the moment he began his kick and was confident of victory. The rest of us followed and I brought up the rear.

We crossed the mile in 4:14 and I was amazed. That was fast, and we still had a whole mile to go. I knew I would die long before the race was over! But we kept going, around and around, Keino still setting the tempo. He picked it up considerably on the seventh lap and it soon became a three-man race, Grelle and I right on Keino's shoulders.

On the straightaway Keino reached for his cap and threw it onto the infield. My immediate thought was, "Boy, if he can keep up his kick from here on in, he can have it!" I wondered if he was serious. Jim Grelle was one of the world's best two-milers and stayed right on Keino, and I desperately tried to keep contact with them. Down the backstretch with 300 yards to go, Keino tried to accelerate but couldn't hold it. I spurted by him in the middle of the final turn, with Grell once more right with me. There we were again, locked into a do-or-die photo finish as we had been so many times before. We were both timed in a new American record 8:25.2, only 2.5 seconds behind Jazy's world mark. I'd held Jim off by the merest of inches.

1. Jim Ryun   8:25.2
2. Jim Grelle   8:25.2
3. Kip Keino   8:29.8
4. Tracy Smith   8:37.4
5. Dyrol Burleson 8:39.6

It was only the second two-mile of my college career;
I was content to settle in behind Keino and Grelle.

When Keino threw off his cap, Grelle and I stayed right
on his shoulder.

In the competition against times, records, and opponents, it can be easy to overlook the personal side of this sport. You can get so locked into winning that you miss very sensitive human dramas being played out in the arena of athletic competition. If those you oppose must always be your adversaries, it is possible to lose out on potentially the greatest rewards of all—the bonds of relationship that form.

It is with fondness that I recall Peter Snell's words of kindness after I had beaten him. A man not given to displays of feeling, he was every inch a gentleman. With almost a gaity my wife and I think back on our evening with Roger Bannister as he delighted us with stories of his family and children; he was a genuine charmer in the classic British tradition. How we enjoyed our visit in Australia with Ron Clarke and his family. There have been those who maintain that a "killer instinct" is the only way to succeed in sport, but that has never been my attitude. One-on-one down the home-stretch, of course you give every ounce you possess to win the race. But it is the relationships that add to and deepen the mystique of the game, relationships that transcend winning and losing.

My frequent stretch-drive battles against Jim Grelle gave me the opportunity to witness a gentleman's character unfold, and it spoke volumes to me about the kind of athlete I wanted to be. So many times I seemed to wind up ahead of Jim by the most infinitesimal of margins. He had every opportunity to be bitter, to resent my displacement of him as America's top miler. Just two weeks after he had broken the American record, I came along and topped it, by a mere .1 of a second. Yet he was always courteous and gracious.

After our battle for third spot on the 1964 Olympic team, I felt I needed to seek him out. I had no idea what to say, but I knew that trip to Tokyo meant a great deal to him. He had already purchased his wife's plane ticket and his was to be as part of the U.S. team. I found him shortly after the race, in some distant corner of the stadium, and awkwardly attempted to share my feelings—not apologizing for beating him but simply expressing my sorrow that it didn't work out for him. We shook hands, with the trace of a tear he wished me luck, and we parted.

We raced many times after that, though age was on my side, and we have remained close friends ever since, knitted together in a mutual respect. Not long ago I received a letter from a young high school runner. He told me he'd once asked Jim Grelle for an auto-

Going over a workout schedule with Coach Timmons in
his office at the University.

With Dr. Roger Bannister in 1967, prior to competition in England.

graph only to be told, "When you get ten Jim Grelle's, you can trade it in for one Jim Ryun." That's the sort of relationship of mutual admiration our rivalry led to.

After a very tiring spring racing season, I was scheduled to participate in one final summer meet in Berkeley that would be the last opportunity of the year to try for a world record in the mile.

I slackened off with the workouts by midweek, doing only several light series of short sprints each day and tapering down to a mere warm-up by week's end. When Saturday came I felt terrific.

I knew I needed help with the pace and three others in the race volunteered. They wanted fast times too; I wanted a good pace but not a rabbit who would burn himself out completely. They were great about it and wanted to help if they could. Tom Von Ruden volunteered to lead the first quarter, Rich Romo the second, and Wade Bell the third. I told them I thought I'd be fine after the half if they could get me there close to 1:56. I asked them to do what they could but not to jeopardize their own races. They wanted four minutes just as badly as I wanted the world record. I was appreciative of how everything was handled and couldn't have done it otherwise.

The meet organizer Sam Bell agreed to downplay the record

With Jim Grelle in 1966 following a race in Los Angeles.

Having a chat with former Kansas mile great Glenn Cunningham following a race.

attempt to minimize the external pressure. When interviewed I made no mention of the record.

The moment finally arrived. When the gun was fired the pace felt easy. Von Ruden led the way. Times were given over the PA system every half lap, and at first I was discouraged thinking we were moving too slowly. As we came out of the second turn of the first lap Romo sped around Von Ruden, who eased back, and I settled into second place. I was surprised to learn the first lap was 57.7. So was the crowd; a low roar of excitement rippled through the stands.

On the second lap I began to worry that maybe we were going *too* fast. Romo had picked it up and we were moving pretty good. Approaching the half-mile Wade Bell took over the lead and I followed him around Romo. The 880 time of 1:55.5 was definitely a record pace and the enthusiasm of the 15,000 spectators began to heighten. I was feeling good. Suddenly the pace slowed into the curve and I knew I could not relax it for long. I realized this was it; from here on it had to be me against the clock.

I surged past Bell and as I assumed the lead I sort of woke up mentally. It was like I'd been in a trance. Now I felt good, glanced over my shoulder, and already could tell the others were falling back. It was an early point to take over the lead, but the clock was unforgiving and I had to push every stride.

I had not started a kick at this stage but lengthened my stride trying to hold a steady pace. When I heard the gun-lap time of 2:55.3 I began to think in terms of 3:50. The crowd was screaming now. Others had come by this fast—Snell had, Jurgen May of Germany had. But both of them died in the final 440.

By now I was tiring, but I knew the record was close. On the backstretch where I ordinarily feel good enough to begin a long drive for home, today I was lacking my usual zip. I tried to pick it up and said to myself, "Sprint!" but it didn't work. I was gradually tying up. The 3:50 idea didn't last long in my mind. Now I was only concerned with finishing and not dying badly. Only one man had ever run this fast for three and a half laps—Herb Elliott, whose Olympic record for 1500 meters of 3:35.6 was the equivalent of a mid-3:51's mile.

Could I do it?

Around the curve, everything that had been my life for the past four years came to focus on me—all those miles, all those cold, lonely morning runs, all those 220's and quarters and 660's on the track, all that sweat in the heat of the Kansas summers. I tried to force my heavy, tired legs to hang on, to pound down the straightaway.

People were jumping up and down, shouting wildly, knowing a record was becoming all the more certain, yelling their encouragement. I drove hard, digging my spikes into the baked clay which flew up behind my spikes, reaching down into my reserves . . . and finally the tape came.

I walked around the curve. Photographers were all over me. The crowd continued its thunderous applause. No one had yet said anything about the time. I was excited and happy. It was something

1. The day of the Berkeley mile race I stayed in my dormitory room all morning, resting and going over my training diary.

2. I stretched . . .

3. Then we lined up and waited for the sound of the gun.

4. Just before the half, Wade Bell took over the pace from Von Ruden and Romo.

5. Now I was all alone and pushed the pace around the third and into the fourth lap.

6. At last I hit the tape!

7. Following the race there were numerous requests for autographs.

I had worked toward a long time. I was not absolutely certain I had done it until the announcement came over the loudspeaker. A new world record!

1. Jim Ryun   3:51.3
2. Cary Weisiger   3:58.0
3. Richard Romo   4:01.4
4. Pat Traynor   4:02.6
5. Tom Von Ruden   4:11.1
6. Wade Bell   4:19.3

CHAPTER 5

Where Do You Go from the Top?

My life after the world record would never be the same. Many intertwining factors would gradually come to bear upon me as a result of what I had achieved. That thrilling afternoon in Berkeley brought to a climax the past four years of running while at the same time it set in motion whole new directions in my life.

Some of the changes began to be evident immediately. Back in my room for scarcely five minutes, I wanted to take a shower and relax. Somehow a reporter had figured out a way to get through to me and pretty soon the phone started ringing.

My friend Neil Steinhauer answered it. "Could I speak with Jim Ryun?" the caller asked.

"He's in the shower," explained Neil, hanging up.

About an hour later, after I was through and dressed, we were sitting around the room and the last thing I wanted was an interview. The phone rang again.

Once more Neil picked it up and heard the same reporter ask for me just as before. "He's in the shower," repeated Neil.

"What! You mean to tell me he's still in the shower?"

"He's a very clean boy," said Neil calmly.

A little later we were watching the "CBS Evening News." Toward the end of the broadcast Walter Cronkite interrupted the regular programming to say, "We have just received this late story from Berkeley, California, where just a few hours ago, young nineteen-year-old Jim Ryun broke the world's record for the one-mile run . . ."

As I sat speechless, and I must admit greatly humbled, and watched a film clip of the race, I was in awe. "What have I done?" I asked myself. "Is this really me who has done this incredible thing? Why . . . I'm part of history!"

However, during the months that followed, I remained largely oblivious to the murmuring winds of change that were subtly beginning to filter through the outer edges of my being, which this brief event only partially began to symbolize. For the time being, I was riding high on the intoxicating crest of being *the* world-record holder in track and field's most glamorous event. After a much-needed summer's rest I was ready to go again. Cross-country season began in the fall and, though I was never a front-runner in the longer races, I thoroughly enjoyed being part of the team knowing the over-distance background was essential for my continued improvement. The next track season wasn't that far away and already I wondered what new challenges it could hold. Everyone was talking 3:50 and I felt my natural progress would make it an easy barrier to pass in time.

But the right moment kept eluding me. Whereas in previous years there had usually been several opportunities to run against opponents who could push me to a fast time, this year it seemed I was always out there alone. It's simply a comment on events as they happened to develop. To run at your optimum, you must not only be pushed with a fast enough pace early in the race, but you also need the emotional stimulation of knowing there is someone potentially better than you right beside you and you must run the race of your life to stay with him. It is impossible to measure the motivation of such forces operating on you. It's this extra charge of adrenalin that makes the difference between a mediocre race and being able to push your body to the ultimate it has to deliver.

Certainly the world was well equipped with a number of milers who could have threatened and even beaten me. The components required for a historic and thrilling race did not jell in any of the mile races I ran that year—opportunity, weather, opposition, my conditioning, and fast early pace.

As the 1967 season wound down, I was entered in the national AAU meet in Bakersfield on June 23. I had been somewhat impatient for a fast mile effort, but, though there was an able field of milers entered, the race was almost certain to have a slow pace since national team positions were at stake and everyone wanted to hold something back for the finish.

By chance I had drawn the inside lane position. Hoping to avoid getting involved in a tight cluster from which I could have been boxed in, bumped, or tripped, I decided to jump right out at the sound of the gun. I then planned to ease back slightly to allow the other runners to move by me, one at a time. I would then be able to settle comfortably into a third or fourth position for the first couple of laps.

The gun went off and I did as planned. Around the curve we went and I began looking back over my shoulder wondering where everyone was. This was unnerving being in the lead so soon!

But no one came, so there I stayed.

The pace was adequate, neither slow nor fast. We passed the 440, the 660. Still I led. And still I was baffled that everyone was content to follow. We crossed the half-mile in 1:59, and I knew the pace was far too slow for a world record. I felt so refreshed I then decided, "Okay, if these guys want to follow, I'll step it up and force the pace. If they want to chase me around the track, I'll make them come and get me!"

I picked up the third lap slightly, crossing the three-quarter mark in just under 2:58. I eased down on the accelerator for a long kick and then it was just a race to the tape. I ran hard and when I crossed the line I was hardly fatigued. There was none of the usual postrace nausea. (My first order of business after most races was to find a bathroom or other solitary spot where, in peace and quiet, I could proceed to lose my lunch.) That evening, most unusual for me, I crossed the line and began almost immediately to talk to the cluster of reporters. It was a remarkably effortless run. I felt so good I thought I'd run in the 3:54 to 3:56 range.

You can imagine my astonishment when I heard my time—.2 under my previous best! Seven runners in all broke four minutes.

1. Jim Ryun   3:51.1
2. Jim Grelle   3:56.1
3. Dave Wilborn   3:56.2
4. Tom Von Ruden   3:56.9
5. Roscoe Divine   3:57.2
6. Sam Bair   3:58.7
7. Marty Liquori   3.59.8

Following the Bakersfield mile, there was considerable excitement when it was learned that I would face Keino, who had been posting some excellent times, in Los Angeles two weeks later (July 9) for the 1967 edition of the U.S. vs. British Commonwealth meet.

Now that the mile mark had fallen twice, it seemed only logical that Herb Elliott's seven-year-old 1500-meter record of 3:35.6

The finish of the Bakersfield AAU mile in 3:51.1.

(considered one of the most phenomenal feats in running history—the equivalent of a 3:51.3 mile in 1960) would be next, especially when Keino and I squared off.

When the day came, the heat down on the floor of the Coliseum was stifling, with the stadium thermometer reading ninety-five degrees. Physically I was ready, but sucking in that air felt like standing in a sauna!

Any world record attempt seemed doomed from the start; none of the runners felt any great urge to take the pace out and the first half-lap was extremely slow. Keino and I followed around past the first quarter mile in just under 61 seconds.

In the Los Angeles 1500 meter, after a first slow quarter, Keino suddenly surged. I flew by the others to keep pace with him.

Keino, however, was never one to fool around with slow paces. Suddenly he streaked to the lead and kept his foot to the floor, racing that second lap in 56 seconds flat. I was right behind him and the two of us left the rest of the field far behind.

I had been perspiring freely even before the gun went off, just from my warm-up. Now in the heat of the race, sweat was pouring from our bodies, chilled by the rush of wind past our faces as we sprinted along the track. I remained a stride behind Keino, locking my eyes on his colorful jersey and trunks. His thin, gliding black legs were but a blur of motion, his spiked shoes kicking up red-brown cinders from the track and peppering them at my trailing knees.

Arms driving, hearts pounding, legs stretching, Keino and I bore down on the track with intensity, oblivious to the 24,000 spectators who had risen to their feet and were by now cheering frantically. There was but the world of each other; we saw nothing else, we heard nothing else.

Keino continued to press the third lap and I followed on his shoulder as we came by in 2:55.0. We were definitely on pace to break Herb Elliott's record. I felt strong, but the question was: Could

Keino and I in the home stretch.

I beat Keino? I'd never seen him run so strong and I knew he would do everything he could to hold me off.

Down the backstretch we drove. I accelerated slightly and eased up alongside him. Side by side we ran, stride for stride. It was a great duel.

This is it, I thought. It's now or never.

I sprinted hard, moved past the African, looked back a couple of times, and then gave it all I was worth. Around the curve and into the homestretch. I'd forgotten the heat, the times, Keino. Up on my toes, I sprinted to the tape, exhausted yet feeling great. When I broke the ribbon, knowing I'd done it, the crowd roared mightily.

1. Jim Ryun   3:33.1
2. Kip Keino   3:37.2
3. Alan Simpson   3:41.7
4. Dave Bailey   3:41.7
5. Jim Grelle   3:43.6
6. Dave Wilborn   3:51.2

I may have felt great *during* the race, but the heat and smog had taxed me to my limit. Immediately after the race I was utterly wasted, hardly able to stand. I staggered around, trying to keep from bumping into reporters who were clustered around taking pictures and shoving microphones into my face. Someone asked about a television interview and I said, "Forget it." My head felt like it had a knife stuck in it three inches, and I had to find some place to get sick! Following a world record, discovering some solitary place where you can bend over in private and throw up is no easy task.

I was far too exhausted to realize the significance of the run. In reporting the race later, *Track & Field News* was very complimentary and put it into perspective:

Ryun moved alongside Keino at three quarters . . . and he looked strong. He raced away from Keino at an almost incredible pace, gaining a yard in every ten.

Jim said, "I really didn't know how fast I was going even after the finish." He had run the last lap in 53.9, his last 880 in 1:51.3. Even more amazing are his calculated times. This was surely his greatest race [the computed equivalent of a 3:48.6 mile!].

Ryun was properly appreciative of Keino's part in setting the record: "Keino's pace definitely helped me." As for Keino . . . he would not comment to the press, but he was heard to exclaim to Naftali Temu, "Oh, that Jim Ryun. He run too *fast.*"

Those who observed Ryun immediately after the race knew he had given his all. He refused an immediate television interview and seemed in distress. [*Track & Field News*, September 1967]

Rising at dawn or earlier for an early morning run had always been part of my schedule. There were numerous times when it was admittedly hard to drag myself out of a warm, cozy bed to endure icy winds, frozen streets, or pounding rains. On the other hand, there was no time of day that more perfectly symbolized the solitary joy and personal triumph of running quite like a long run in those quiet hours when the rest of the world slept.

My morning runs were often the highlight of a trip to a new place, and I especially found this true when I traveled abroad. What a magnificent way to sightsee in a strange city, whether it was San Francisco, London, New York, Sydney, or Kiev. Walking through the lobby of a hotel at 5:30 in the morning in running trunks caused double takes by more than one night desk clerk, but once out in the streets, I was free to enjoy the time of my life. No schedule, no deadline, no one pestering me. I just ran and ran in whatever directions looked interesting—up hills to gain a bird's-eye view, through deserted old streets and alleys, along the main arteries, past famous landmarks, across the Golden Gate Bridge, along the Champs Élysées, through a redwood forest, down New York's Fifth Avenue. If we were competing against a rival university, I would often run through the campus and perhaps by the stadium. Throughout the course of a six- or eight-mile run, the city gradually awoke and began stirring itself into action for the coming day. It felt good inside to have been part of that coming-to-life process.

Late in the summer of 1967 came a trip to Europe with the U.S. track team, during which time I enjoyed many such early rambles through scenic European cities and countrysides. In Dusseldorf, West Germany, I ran against Harold Norpoth, Bodo Tummler, and Jim Grelle in one of my most memorable tactical races. The field was small, the crowd clearly partisan in favor of their German favorites, and any one of us capable of winning. After three laps in which Jim Grelle and I alternated with the lead, the stage was set for a mad dash to the tape. Cordner Nelson of *Track & Field News* recorded it as follows:

With four of the fastest finishers of all time in the battle, the pace was extremely slow. At the bell, Tummler jumped into the lead, while Norpoth delayed Ryun. But Ryun swung around Norpoth on the curve, with the German crowd roaring loudly.

Then came the fastest burst of speed ever recorded in any mile or 1500-meter race. Ryun accelerated so fast and left Tummler behind so rapidly that the German crowd was stunned into silence. One expert observer timed Ryun's 100 meters along the backstretch in a nearly incredible 11.6 seconds.

In the early stages of the Dusseldorf 1500 meter as I followed Tummler and Norpoth.

After a 50-second final 400 I pulled away from the two Germans and fellow American Jim Grelle.

Ryun continued to pull away . . . His last 400 was the fastest on record
—50.6. (One report gave his last 400 as 49.7.)

Ryun finished the season with a clear-cut superiority in speed over all
other milers in history. [Cordner Nelson and Robert Quercetani, *Runners
and Races* (Los Altos, Calif.: Tafnews Press, 1973), p. 277]

Most memorable about the summer, however, were not the races
but my run-ins with the aggressive overseas media. I was hounded
by reporters from morning till night. The American press had always been very courteous to me, never downright rude. But in
Europe I discovered it to be otherwise.

In London I had been so harassed that I simply had to get away.
A writer for *Sports Illustrated,* my friend Rich Clarkson, who was
doing photo work for them at the time, and I planned to drive to
Henley-on-the-Thames for a break.

A London newspaper had been determined to get an interview
with me, complete with photo coverage. By this time I was equally
determined to resist. They'd stationed a photographer outside my
hotel and when we walked out to begin our drive up the river for
lunch, he started clicking pictures madly. We got into our car. He
got into his and proceeded to follow us through the streets, pulling
as close alongside as he could, still clicking away—this time through
the car windows! We drove first to the apartment where the *Sports
Illustrated* reporter was staying. Up behind us pulled the very annoy-
ing photographer from the newspaper; he parked and waited for us.

It had almost at this point turned into a game, a highly challenging one. Leaving the apartment, we determined to shake this guy if
it took every James Bond ploy in the book. We jumped into our
rented European compact and took off. He was right behind us.

Through the streets of London we sped, made all the more
harrowing because we were trying to lose an experienced Briton
while driving on the left-hand side of the road. It's a miracle we
didn't wind up in a heap! Right turns . . . left turns . . . in and out
of the traffic at breakneck speed. Still he clung to us. Sudden
changes of course down narrow alleys, behind warehouses, even
stopping to make quick 180-degree reversals. Nothing worked. The
guy could not be shaken!

Eventually we found ourselves out in the country, speeding
along, still relentlessly pursued. The road was narrow and two lane.
Climbing a hill we came upon a slow-moving truck, passed it
quickly, and were relieved to see an oncoming stream of traffic in

the other lane, rendering it temporarily impossible for our tail to get by the truck until cresting the hill. Pushing the accelerator down, at the top of the hill we encountered a fork in the road and we immediately pulled off the main highway and careened down the dirt road with reckless abandon, winding up suddenly in front of what appeared to be a huge country estate or mansion.

We stopped and waited. Had we lost him?

We scarcely had time to think about him, however, because almost immediately from out of the house charged three of the most enormous dogs I have ever seen. Crammed helplessly inside a very tiny car, we struggled frantically to roll up the windows so that when the dogs reached us we were—well, if not safe, at least quarantined from them. I thought they were going to eat the car as they jumped up on it, pawing at us through the windows, and raised such an uproar. But no one came out of the house to arrest us for trespassing and after ten or fifteen minutes it was clear we'd shaken the reporter.

Gingerly we started up the car, backed up the road, left the dogs behind, and enjoyed a very pleasant lunch and afternoon at Henley-on-the-Thames.

I encountered a very insistent German newsman in Dusseldorf, so insistent that he followed me onto the track just five minutes before the race was to begin, wanting an interview *right then*. I couldn't get loose from the guy and could not help feeling very perturbed with him.

The race had not been over long when there he came again to hound me. Still catching my breath, I continued to walk around the infield while he—half beside me, half in front—pummeled me with questions. As I walked and did my best to respond, he kept moving also, walking backwards in order to keep facing me.

Somehow my usual kind and gracious nature was less than operative that day, and I failed to mention the approaching disaster awaiting him to his rear as we neared one end of the grassy infield. A few seconds later he lay sputtering and drenched in the steeplechase water jump.

End of interview.

CHAPTER 6

Changing Times

The winds of change in my life were gradually accelerating. Forces were gathering momentum that would ultimately overturn this youngster-turned-hero fairy tale that had characterized my life till now.

I'd been running almost five years. I had begun as a clumsy and insecure junior high kid and now I was on the summit, standing alone as the fastest middle-distance runner of all time. Most historic milestones have a way of forever altering those inaugurating them. The moment a man or woman steps boldly into the flow of history, his life is no longer his own. He is swept up in forces greater than himself and is often powerless to change the tide of their motion.

My life after 1967 was dramatically altered. Every aspect of my being took on new and more complex dimensions. What you have been reading up to this point—a more-or-less factual account of my first twenty years—has in a sense been introductory to the true story of my life. For during these early years of running, as I've mentioned, there was a sense in which I lived a sheltered life inside a bubble where there was only one thing to do—run. If I worked hard, I would get better, I would win, and eventually I could become the best. Moreover, being the best would ultimately yield the fulfill-ment in life I longed for—the feeling of esteem, personal worth, and belonging. During these teen years, psychologists have reported that there are three basic needs that must be met—those of accept-ance, achievement, and affection. I was in search of all three. Such goals were sufficient to keep me training, working, running, and winning. I was young, didn't deeply analyze the flow of my life, and simply kept pace with what I assumed was the path that would lead to ultimate happiness in life.

But unavoidably because of what I had now achieved at such a tender age, I was thrust into a position where the simplicity of my former life could never survive. The bubble that had protected me began slowly to disintegrate.

There were a number of crucial factors in this. Perhaps foremost was simply the matter of internal motivation. It is impossible to overstate the mental and emotional contribution to athletic excellence. Certainly God endowed me with a unique body, and I am the first to admit that my athletic deeds are founded in no particular meritorious achievement for which I should be lauded. Many athletes have worked as hard as I. Yet we are each responsible within ourselves to make something of what we have been given. I was motivated and trained diligently. The better my performances, the stronger my internal motives, the harder I worked. As I matured and strengthened and as the potential rewards grew greater—world records, gold medals, winning against the world's best—I literally became a running machine. It is impossible to run forty repeat quarters or toil through sixteen miles in the rain without immense inner drive.

It is inevitable that such an intensity can only be sustained for so long. I'd certainly progressed further than I'd ever dreamed. So where do you go next? Once you're on top, where do you find a new mountain to climb?

Certainly there were hosts of things I hadn't done—a 3:50 mile, a world record two-mile, and so on. But anyone becomes hard-pressed to pump himself back up mile after mile, race after race, year after year, to pursue such goals, especially in the wake of the tremendous emotional release of what had already happened. I ran between 30 and 50 races a year, which amounted to something over 300 races by the end of my career. It is just an emotional impossibility to sustain over such an extended stretch of time that tingle of newness that excites and keeps you going in the early days of some new endeavor.

It has been hypothesized that every world-class athlete has a certain time in his or her life when he has a shot at it "all"—a period when physical, emotional, and psychological factors all perfectly converge and blend with circumstances and competition. At that one period of life, things click and a personal summit is reached. Everything crystallizes just right. Although some remain at that level longer than others, it has been historically shown that it is

impossible to sustain it forever. Even though physical maturity and abilities may remain in peak condition for up to twenty years, very few performers stay on the top for more than three, four, or five years. Because so much more than physical conditioning is involved.

There were many who now began to voice doubts about my future. Former indoor mile world-record holder Tom O'Hara said he didn't feel it was possible for me to keep up the mental pace much longer than I already had. Asked bluntly if he thought my career was coming to an end, O'Hara answered, "Yes." In an interview published in the *Wichita Eagle,* he went on:

This is a mental thing and I think a man can take it three or four years at the most. Maybe five years, but you just can't take that—including the 100 miles of practice per week—forever. The mental part of it is definitely harder to keep going than the physical part. If you don't keep that intense desire, it is useless, and I don't think you can keep it longer than four or five years.

It was not that my desire to excel abruptly flagged. Always fiercely intent on doing my best, I was assiduously driven toward success at the upcoming Mexico City Olympic Games. In my career, though there'd been acclaim and age-group, high school, national, and now even world records along the way, there had yet loomed one notable moment of failure—my Olympic performance in 1964. Before my career could be considered "complete," there was that single unachieved token of glory that every track-and-field athlete dreams of, the one symbol of recognition known the world over that says "Among all men, *you* are the best!"—the Olympic gold medal.

It would be inaccurate to imply that my desire was dulled. I *wanted* that gold medal with everything I had. I dreamed of it! I felt I had the "raw material" to run faster. Timmie and I had discussed, in very concrete terms, a 3:30 1500 and a 3:46 mile. Such thoughts did not awe me; I knew they were reachable—physically. The ease of my 3:33.1 against Keino on a relatively slow cinder track on a hot day gave me great confidence in my capabilities.

However, the single-minded devotion to running that had been the hallmark of the past five years simply could not last. It became more and more difficult to channel my desire for the gold medal into a daily enthusiasm for training. My self-disciplined temperament enabled me to continue working toward the objective. Yet the fervor was subsiding. Running was the only life I had known for five years now, but a drudgery was gradually setting in. After some 15,000 to 20,000 miles and between 2,500 and 3,000 hours of running, it was no longer fresh and invigorating.

Day in and day out, my life was in a rut. At 5:30 the alarm went off and I dragged myself out of bed, groggily suited up, and went out for a morning run. Everyone else was still asleep and it was dark outside. But every morning there I was, running through the streets of Lawrence or in the surrounding countryside. After a while it all looked the same.

Through the day I attended my classes, studied in the library, and went to the track at 2:30 for the afternoon workout. By the time I had dinner at the cafeteria and climbed the tall flight of stairs to my dormitory room, it was dark once more. I plopped down on my bed for a rest before getting in a few hours of studying before bedtime.

And then the cycle began all over again.

Not only was I tired of the monotony, there were so many people and forces vying for my attention. In no way could I give everyone what they expected. In the beginning Timmie had been nearly the only force operating in my life. Now there were hundreds of people, each wanting a little slice of me for something.

Accompanying all this was the starved public appetite for more

For as long as I've run, the morning run has been part of my routine. While attending the University, I was usually up before the city was awake to run through the streets toward the surrounding countryside.

While in New York City I have run through Central Park.

There is no greater way to become familiar with a new city—in this case, the French Quarter of New Orleans—than to experience its early-morning quiet.

The sweet-smelling solitude of a run through a quiet pine forest, near Flagstaff, Ariz.

There are the days when it's so hot that the sweat is dripping off. . . . Volcano rubble in Flagstaff, Ariz., near San Francisco Peaks.

. . . and others when perspiration freezes in the wrinkles of your sweat suit. Taken in combination, such runs make one hearty and mentally tough.

On the *Today* show with host Hugh Downs and Joe Garagiola.

. . . more . . . more! I recognize this as a natural phenomonon and I certainly bear neither the press nor the public any ill feeling about it. My youthful and rapid rise to the top had made of me, in some circles at least, almost a folk hero. People always expect wondrous feats from their heroes. Heroes are not viewed as mortals, with needs, emotions, and frailties.

I am grateful to the press. The media had usually been very gracious to me and most complimentary. I developed a number of close friendships with news personnel. I'd been on the cover of *Sports Illustrated* seven times, *Track & Field News* I don't know how many times, and even *Newsweek*. That year, 1966, I received the *Sports Illustrated* Sportsman's Award, the AAU Sullivan Award, the ABC Sports Award, and others. All in all, the point is that I received very favorable press.

Because of this ground swell of praise for my accomplishments, written up regularly in publications ranging from church bulletin editorials to the *Wall Street Journal,* two factors emerged. One, there was an almost obsessive fascination with my personal life, subjecting me to unimaginably detailed scrutiny. Two entire books were written—independently of me—that delved into everything, from what I ate to where I studied to what girl I may have been interested

Receiving the *Sports Illustrated* "Sportsman of the Year" Award for 1966. From left to right: Jim Grelle, Wes Santee, Glenn Cunningham, Rafer Johnson, Bobby Morrow, Jim Ryun, and Billy Mills.

in to how I tied my shoes, probing thoughts I'd scarcely been asked about.

And then there was the perpetual expectation to reach further, to run faster. It was as if they all said, "You are our champion. Now we are counting on even more magnificent things from you."

The pressure was not intentional, to be sure. Everyone was proud of me and pulling for me. Although the public adulation was not without its momentary gratification, it slowly worked its way under my skin where it grew into a silent burden to perform to the levels the whole country anticipated.

After the Berkeley mile, every interview focused on "When do you anticipate breaking the 3:50 mile?" That was all that was spoken of. Therefore, the Bakersfield run, even though there had never been a mile so fast in history, was greeted almost with disappointment in the press. It was good, they said, but . . . well, it was so close and wouldn't it have been greater *if . . .?* It was never said in so many words, but subtly I could sense that people had expected more from *the* Jim Ryun. Following the 3:51.1, on a televised interview on "Wide World of Sports," the whole emphasis was on what I *hadn't* done rather than on what I *had* accomplished. The once golden boy of stage and screen, the kid everyone was pulling for, was now at the seasoned age of twenty falling subject to the more negative scrutiny of the fickle public thirst for perfection.

Ultimately, the expectations—both of the public and those I placed on myself—prohibited me from enjoying the simple pleasures of running itself: experiencing the solitude of a Kansas field, stopping to talk to a group of cows, standing victorious on top of a hard-fought hill, exulting in the changing seasons of the country-side, seeing the sweat pouring off your sun-drenched chest on a hot summer day, feeling what seems to be a sanctified stillness while running through a gentle snowfall, absorbing the sights and pleasures of an unfamiliar city at 5:30 in the morning, sprinting hard alongside a friend at the end of an arduous run not knowing whether to cry from the pain or to laugh because it's so much fun. These were no longer what running meant to me.

CHAPTER 7

Anne

After the world-record run in July of 1966 at Berkeley, when I had finally shaken what seemed like a thousand hands, signed a hundred autographs, and answered fifty reporters' questions, I worked myself free from the crowds and headed back to the dorm where I had been staying. I jogged back barefoot because in the aftermath of the race, while I was being hounded in every direction by the crowds, someone had taken souvenir hunting to the extreme and stolen my shoes. Exultant from the race, I was nevertheless weary from the constant press of people and a little perturbed about my shoes. Thus when three more people stopped me as I left the stadium and asked for an autograph, I waved them off brusquely, saying, "I've signed all I can for one day. Can't you get it later?" I kept jogging to my room and promptly forgot the incident altogether.

Five months later and 2,000 miles away the East High track team was planning a reunion on Thanksgiving day. One of my close friends, a student at Kansas State in Manhattan, Kansas (about eighty miles from the University of Kansas in Lawrence), asked me if I'd like to have a blind date for the reunion party with a girl he knew from Kansas State.

"Sure," I said. "Why not?"

So there I was that Thanksgiving evening, driving up to a large brownstone house where the two girls were staying for a date with a girl I'd never met. We walked up to the door, knocked, and were shown in.

"Jim," my friend said when the girls came down, "meet Anne Snider. Anne, this is Jim Ryun."

I looked down to see a tiny young lady, with flashing hazel eyes and a wide smile that never left her face. Her short-cropped, blond hair reminded me of a pixy, and from the moment she opened her mouth, so did her winning personality.

"Hi!" said Anne buoyantly. "It's really exciting to meet you. All my family loves sports and my brothers are great fans of yours."

"Thank you," I said modestly. I never did figure out how to respond to statements like that.

"We were at Berkeley, you know," she went on.

"Last summer?" I asked.

"Yes. We saw your 3:51."

"What were you doing there?"

"I was with my parents visiting my sister in California. My youngest brother had some tickets to the meet, and so we went. To tell you the truth," Anne said, stopping for a high-spirited laugh in mid-sentence, "before that I hadn't really followed your career that much."

I said nothing.

"But let me tell you," she continued, "after that race I became your greatest fan. It was fantastic!" Another laugh followed.

"Thanks," I said again, feeling a bit awkward.

"Let's go sit down in the living room," someone suggested.

"I tried to get your autograph," Anne said.

"Tried?"

"It was after the race and my sister, brother, and I stopped you on the campus outside the stadium. You weren't in too much of a talking mood and told us to get it some other time. You were barefoot."

"My shoes had just been swiped," I said.

Anne laughed. "Jim Ryun's shoes stolen? What a kick!"

I forced a small laugh. This girl is really something, I thought to myself. She cracks up over every little thing.

"Could I get it now?"

"What?"

"Your autograph," Anne said giggling. "You said to get it later. And so now I'm asking for it—an official request."

"Well . . . I . . . I suppose," I said, glancing about me. Anne handed me several pieces of paper for not one but a dozen autographs, I signed my name hurriedly, and that was that!

The ice was broken, and we sat and talked for another several minutes before we got up to drive to the track party. Anne talked and laughed the whole time. I made every effort to do all the right things—open the doors at the proper time, walk on the right side, and so on—but I'm afraid the conversation was slightly one-sided. I later learned that the moment we had walked out of the house, Mrs. Booth had run to the kitchen, grabbed a wad of cellophane, wrapped it around the cushion where I had been sitting on the couch, and placed a note on top of it that read "Jim Ryun sat here!"

I will never forget the rest of that evening. In my memory it remains as clear as yesterday. For Anne was incredible—so sparkling, gay, and full of life—with a happy, childlike joy that erupted out of her every minute or two. Anne's bouncing personality was not significant so much for what it was in itself, but for what it represented in contrast to *my* personality. I had always been known as a soft-spoken, retiring, straitlaced sort of guy and now here I was paired up with Miss Personality herself. It was a mismatch if ever there was one. Not to mention that I was 6′3″ and she was 5′3″. My father found this differential so hilarious that he later built Anne a pair of stilts to make up the difference.

By the time we arrived at the track party, Anne had succeeded in loosening me up a bit, and I was having a good time.

"Hey, Ryun!" I heard when we walked in, and immediately I was plunged into all the track talk that was so much a part of such gatherings—questions about my races and records, recounting of the stories of our high school years, and so on. And there Anne was, right in the middle of it, laughing, talking, and playing the perfect "life of the party" role. I had to admit to myself that this blind date had so far worked out pretty well.

The evening went on. We played pool there at the house and then someone said, "Hey, let's go get some pizza."

We piled in the cars and took off for the pizza parlor. The whole time, though I was talking and goofing around with the other guys, a part of me was standing back watching this young lady I was with. For one thing, she laughed at everything! But I could tell it wasn't phony. It was just an exuberance she felt; she enjoyed life. Another thing that struck me was how much she liked people and was able to enter into their lives.

By the time we were sitting around the table eating our pizza, Anne had become everyone's friend.

"Anne," one of my friends called out from the other end of the table, "you're from K. State, right?"

The future Mrs. Jim Ryun leading a cheer at Kansas State University.

"You bet!" said Anne, "And proud of it!" There followed a laugh.

"Do you know Dee Gadberry?"

"Oh sure. We're in the same sorority. In fact, she's my pledge daughter."

"Sorority sisters—loyalty, tradition, and all that stuff?" chimed another.

Before she could answer, the first guy asked, "Could you fix me up with her?"

"A date?" said Anne.

He nodded.

"No way, buster!" said Anne, laughing again. Then she added, to the delight of everyone else at the table, among whom this particular runner's reputation with young ladies was well known, "I let people get into their own trouble all by themselves! I fix no one up . . . except myself, of course."

While all the others were laughing at her good-natured put-down, Anne looked up at me. Our eyes met and somehow I knew her last words had been meant for me. This girl was really something!

I can hardly answer for what it was like for Anne to have a date with Mr. Dull. But something changed for me that night. Someone had opened a door and let the sunlight into what was becoming a very dreary existence. The moment I met Anne, it was like someone had taken the blinders off and, lo and behold, there was a world out there—to be enjoyed. And the fact that this messenger of life and good cheer came in such a bright, bubbly, energetic package . . . It was exciting, and I was smitten!

Thanksgiving over, Anne returned to Kansas State and I to Lawrence, where my preparations for Mexico City were steadily intensifying. My class schedule was heavy and my workouts had never been so difficult and demanding.

Suddenly I had something other than running to think of. I found myself during the day lapsing into daydreams in the middle of class. Now my mind wasn't resting solely on the gold medal and that afternoon's workout on the track. In addition, there was an image of a pretty, smiling face that was, even at this moment, sitting in a class somewhere eighty miles away.

After that wonderful Thanksgiving Day, I wasn't about to let Anne go. I began to call her occasionally. The calls grew more regular and longer. Then I started to drive over to see her in my '64 Plymouth whenever I had a weekend free. As the racing season progressed, Anne began to come to Lawrence more often, since I was unable to get away. More and more of my thoughts became focused on her and our increasingly serious relationship. The single dimension of running that had represented my life for so long was now split down the middle. No longer was running my only concern; I had other interests, other loves. Anne grew to occupy an equal place with running and I had to balance priorities in two separate areas.

My life was fuller, my workouts tougher, evenings longer, and the time for rest and sleep shorter. The hour-and-a-half drives between Manhattan and Lawrence had to be sandwiched between so many other things and often came late at night.

The two halves of me were living completely distinct lives. All day I toiled through classes and workouts. Timmie had me on a rugged schedule because we knew Mexico City would be the supreme challenge of my running career. So on most days when I suited up at the stadium and then headed out for the track to warm up, I knew I would put in twenty or thirty or sometimes forty repeats between a 220 and a half-mile in length. While a small part of me wanted to hurry through these workouts, I knew if I did that all would be lost. The goal of Mexico City and a gold medal still loomed in the forefront of my mind.

Because of the demanding training schedule, I saw Anne mostly on weekends. When with her, a great calm came over me. The pressures and anxieties of my running self vanished. I became another person. I put running completely out of my mind and simply relaxed in her presence. She opened whole new worlds for me. I had always been so quiet and now I was with someone who was not only a great conversationalist but who drew me out as well. We talked and talked and talked, about anything and everything. We were intensely interested in one another. If we hadn't been together in a week, it seemed it took two hours of rapid interaction just to get caught up—how are classes going, what's happening at K. State or K.U., what are you feeling and thinking about? We talked a lot about religion, even though at this point neither of us had a personal faith of our own. Anne (who had been brought up Episcopalian) and I were worlds apart as to our ideas of who God was, who Jesus was, and how they fit into our daily lives.

Occasionally we went out on "dates," to dinner or a movie. Mostly we just spent time together doing what we normally did, and always talking. The process was so broadening for me, opening wider dimensions in my awareness. Anne became my sounding board. I would tell her things I would never have said to anyone else, certainly not to the press, not to my parents, not even to Timmie. Back in my dormitory room alone, Anne remained in my thoughts. I might write a note or letter, or make a collage plaque for her. Let's face it—I was in love!

Many times we would study together in the library, either at K.

Anne and I horsing around at Pillsbury Landing near Manhattan, Kansas.

State or K.U., wherever we happened to be at the time. I often wonder how much studying we actually got done. It was just an excuse to be together. We'd wander around the vast shelves of books trying to find a solitary corner table someplace where we could open our books, get out a pencil, and then proceed to whisper and giggle. Occasionally we had to buckle down and get some serious work done. More often than not, we left the library early, wandered down the back stairway and outside, horsing around with each other, laughing, and wandering about the campus. Often on Sundays we went out to dinner together, if I could scrape up any money (I was always broke; my scholarship paid my fees but that's all), or went on long walks through the streets of town.

Anne remained oblivious to my "second" life of running. She had no concept of the intensity involved. Since my life with her provided a much-needed escape from the mounting pressure, I rarely spoke with her about it. I managed to keep the divided halves almost entirely segregated.

I was burning the candle at both ends and anyone with an ounce of insight could have seen that it could not last. Unfortunately, I did not see it. From around the edges of my life there began to filter in a growing criticism of my relationship with Anne. After all, these well-meaning counselors reasoned, if I was to achieve the heights for which I was destined, a moonstruck heart and crisscrossing Kansas for late-night meetings would only work against me. Single-ness of purpose, with running at its core, was the only way toward ultimate success and victory.

Unfortunately, I had been immersed in that lopsided lifestyle too long and wasn't about to let go of the most exciting person I had ever met.

One of my close friends saw these two parts of me steadily diverging and was aware of the enormous pressures that came to bear on the running part of my life. He took me aside one day and simply said, "Jim, you really better make sure you know what you're doing."

He was right, of course. There were dangers and I was oblivious to them. Even if I had seen them, I wouldn't have changed anything. So my natural response was, "Stick it in your ear, fella!"

I simply hoped I would be able to hang on until Mexico City in October. After that my running life could relax considerably.

After a year and a half together, in May of 1968, Anne and I became engaged.

CHAPTER 8

Preparation for Mexico City

When Mexico City, was selected as the site for the XIX Olympiad, few suspected the mere location would prove more responsible for the long-term effects of the Games than the millions of dollars and hours spent by the world's athletes in preparation. Prior to Mexico City, altitude running had scarcely been considered. We tossed around the term *oxygen debt* knowing that when you run at high speeds your body's muscles consume oxygen faster than your lungs can replenish it. We scarcely anticipated that running where the oxygen content of the air was substantially less would dramatically alter this replenishing process. No one really understood how oxygen debt, rarified air, and running intertwined. In a manner befitting their wisdom and adaptability, when the question "Will the altitude be a factor?" was posed before a meeting of the International Olympic Committee in 1963, the Mexican representative stood and answered simply, "No." And that ended the discussion.

In early 1967, after an NCAA Indoor Championship Meet, I was collared by Kansas State steeplechaser Conrad Nightingale who took me to meet a man by the name of Jack Daniels, then working on his doctorate at the University of Wisconsin on the effects of altitude on athletic performance. Daniels wanted to talk to me, he said, and did I have some time? It was important.

Jack got straight to the point. "You know, Ryun," he began, "that altitude in Mexico is going to be a serious problem and you'd better start preparing for it."

At first I was casual in my response. "I'll work hard," I said. "I'll be sure to arrive in top condition."

"Being in shape won't matter," replied Daniels. "You have to acclimate yourself to the effects of altitude. Actually, that's a misnomer. You *can't* acclimatize yourself. All you can do is reduce the impact of the problem. No matter how hard you work at sea level, you can't accomplish the same thing."

"My coach doesn't think there's anything to worry about," I said.

"I don't care what he or anyone else says," Daniels insisted. "I've conducted experiments. I've written letters, published my findings. But no one's listening. The U.S. Olympic Committee—"

He stopped, shaking his head in frustration.

"A lot of people are going to be hurt, that's all I'm going to say."

"What if they're right?" I suggested. "I mean if they're all saying there's nothing to worry about."

"These Olympic officials haven't studied this thing. They don't know anything about altitude! And I tell you, you sea-level guys are going to have trouble. In anything over 800 meters, it could be disastrous for us. And, Ryun, the 1500 could be the worst of all."

"How so?" I asked.

"Oxygen debt. There just won't be enough oxygen for sea-level runners to perform anywhere near optimum levels. It will affect the 5,000, 10,000, steeplechase, and marathon. The times will be slow and the recovery horrendous."

"So what makes the 1500 so special?"

"This is just a theory, you understand, but in the 1500 you have stamina and speed converging at a very concentrated point. In the longer races, because the speeds are slower, the oxygen debt won't be as severe. But in the near-sprint pace of the 1500, it's going to be unbelievable. Even if you show up in the condition of your life, I doubt you'll do better than a four-minute pace. I wouldn't be surprised if 3:38 won it. And that'll be one of the Africans who's been used to it all his life. I tell you, Ryun, it's going to feel like someone stuck a knife in your lungs with a lap to go. You're going to try to sprint and it'll be like nothing you've ever experienced. You may be the world's best at sea level. But over 7,000 feet, you'll feel like you were back in junior high."

Daniels was serious, and he had certainly caught my attention.

"So how do we prepare then?" I asked.

"You've got to train over 7,000 feet. Not because your body can adapt, but just to get used to how it feels. The key is to start a race slower than you're used to. Too fast a pace and you'll see sea-level runners dropping like flies. Tell you what," suggested Daniels, him-

Jack Daniels advising Conrad Nightingale and me about our altitude training program.

self a former Olympic medalist. "Come to Alamosa with me. That's in Colorado at 7,400 feet. I'm working there with some of the other guys. All I ask is that you hear me out, maybe run a test or two, see how you feel. What have you got to lose?"

With this beginning Daniels finally persuaded me to stop by his training center on my way back to Kansas from the Compton Invitational track meet in early June. Jack arranged a one-mile time trial with some of the others present. We started at a relatively slow pace. At a lap and a half I felt awful! My chest was heaving and I couldn't get my breath. I simply could not continue.

I pulled up and stopped, thoroughly convinced about altitude.

After a twenty- or thirty-minute break, I said to Jack, "This is ridiculous. I came here to run a mile and I'm not going to quit after a slow 660. Let's try it again."

I was fit. I'd just run an easy 3:53 in Los Angeles a few days earlier and physically was prepared to bust one.

So off we all went again, a bit more cautiously. This time I finished—in 4:32. It was *not* a piece of cake as the 3:53 had been. I felt about ready to die!

I needed no further persuasion. I immediately altered my summer plans so I could train with Jack there in Alamosa for several weeks, paying my way bagging groceries for a local supermarket.

Jack's contention was not that by training at altitude we could actually hope to gain any ground on the problem or in any sense "overcome" it. There was no way to do that. He agreed with Dr. Roger Bannister (the world's first sub-four-minute miler) who, interviewed later, responded to the question "What would it take to become thoroughly acclimated to altitude?"

"There are two ways," Bannister said simply. "Be born at altitude . . . or train there for twenty-five years."

Everything we did in Colorado confirmed Jack's warnings. The preparation improved recovery and at least accustomed us to the unique form of pain involved. But it never actually enabled us to run *faster* at altitude. As Dr. Bannister pointed out, it would take a lifetime for the human body to physiologically adapt to the point that it could utilize less oxygen to produce an equivalent output. That was something we could never hope to achieve.

Jack drove us to the Great Sand Dunes National Monument, which contains dunes like you've never seen. Running up steep, loose sand is difficult enough at sea level, but after several miles of torturous dunes at 8,000 feet, the chest pain is phenomenal.

On another occasion, having no idea what I was getting into, Jack said, "Okay, today we're running the pass."

"Oh no," moaned several of the others who had been there longer than I. "Anything but the pass!"

"Come on," said Jack. "It's only seven miles.

"How bad can a seven-mile jaunt be?" I said.

"Bad, Ryun, let me tell you—*bad!*" said one of my fellow runners.

"Oh, Ryun," said another sarcastically, "you're going to love this one. This is one that you'll want to read about in all the newspapers. Boy, *Sports Illustrated* would love to get ahold of this. Where is that photographer anyway? He should be here getting a 'before' and 'after' shot of this workout!"

"You're going to think someone reached down your throat and turned your lungs inside out," said another. "You've heard of the shoot-out at Apache Flat? Well let me tell you, this place ain't flat!"

"We call it 'runners dying in Moccasin Pass,' " said Jack with a laugh.

Though we were staying at 7,400 feet already, we piled into our cars and drove up *another* 1,100 feet to the sand dunes about thirty miles from Alamosa. Jack pulled off the road and turned off the engine.

"Well guys, this is it. Everybody out!"

Noticeably reluctant, we obeyed.

He started the stopwatch, we took off, and Jack drove on ahead to wait at the finish. It may have been only seven miles, but what he failed to tell me was that in that short distance the elevation climbed from 8,500 feet to 11,000.

That was a run unlike anything I'd ever experienced. My ears were shot through with pain, my lungs had a thousand little knives stuck in them, and as I gasped for air, there just didn't seem to be any relief. There was no oxygen to be had! By the time we staggered toward the finish, I was moving at about a nine-minute-mile pace, my legs were numb, and I wanted an oxygen mask.

After my few weeks at Alamosa in 1967, I was genuinely apprehensive as I anticipated Mexico. There would be no opportunities to do extended altitude work during the school year. Therefore I saw my only choice in preparing for Mexico to be to work that much harder. Altitude training or not, the better shape I was in, the faster I'd be capable of running.

I'd always been a hard worker. When training away from home, there were times other coaches instructed their runners to stay away from me—I'd work them too hard. As the 1967–68 year opened I bore down all the more. I continued to train twice a day, but with greatly increased intensity. Where before I would have rested perhaps every other day with a light ten-mile run, now I pushed myself to my maximum limit every day. Coming right off a hard previous day's workout and a six- to eight-mile run that morning, I would crank up for twenty quarters in 60 seconds, or maybe thirty in 65 seconds. Every time I suited up I ran hard. Every chance I drove myself to the limit.

During that winter, I felt strong as a horse. The work was paying off; I was in the condition of my life. Everything seemed to be progressing on schedule toward the Olympics.

But like the mythical character whose fatal flaw proves his undoing, it was these very workouts—designed to make me stronger —that ultimately broke me down.

I was seeing Anne with increased frequency and carrying a heavy class load as well. Driving to and from Manhattan to visit Anne, training early every morning and hard each afternoon, squeezing in classes and studies every free moment even if it sometimes meant I got to bed later than usual, cutting my sleep short— all of these factors eventually proved too much. In quest of the gold

Dragging myself up one of the monstrous sand dunes at Colorado's Great Sand Dunes National Monument.

High-altitude distance work near Moccasin Pass, Colo.

High-altitude distance work. Distance running near Adams' State College, Alamoca, Colo.

medal I pushed myself too far. I had worked *too* hard, without sufficient rest, and my body could not take the stress. I had tried to cram too many activities into a schedule where there was simply no more room.

The first serious injury came in March. During a workout involving some very fast 110s, suddenly a hamstring popped. The two-week layoff set me back more severely than usual, and even after the rest I was tired. I could feel myself dragging during workouts and suddenly the results began to fall off badly and the fatigue worsened.

In late May, after a series of blood tests, the trouble was discovered—I had mononucleosis. Not only did the news devastate my Olympic plans and hoped-for high-altitude training, it was an embarrassing diagnosis. Here I had just three days earlier become engaged to Anne, and now the news leaked out that I had mono! Who was going to realize that with my body's defenses being down, I could have just as easily caught it walking across the campus? No, this was too rich for that, and how the tongues wagged when they heard. "Ryun's all washed up now," they said. "Forget about Mexico City!" Inevitably, such negative inquiries could not help but direct themselves toward Anne, even if little was explicitly said. No longer did I represent the fair-haired American boy who could do no wrong. I had grown up, got myself in a pickle, and was liable to blow it if I wasn't careful.

It was subtle, but the winds of fortune were shifting.

The Olympics drew nearer and remained clouded in controversy. Talk grew of a boycott by America's black athletes to protest racial discrimination in the United States. Altitude was being discussed more and more heatedly.

I rested for three weeks after the blood tests, then began easing back into slow running and gradually worked into some speed work. A twisted ankle in early July cost me four days of training. Later in the month I battled a nasty flu bug—several more days missed. My bodily systems were still struggling, and I found myself exhausted after only three or four days of hard training. I could not take a fraction of the work load I'd long been accustomed to. Always in the back of my mind remained the phantom of Kip Keino, born and bred in the Kenyan highlands.

The Olympic Trial finals were to be held at Lake Tahoe, and I'd decided to try both the 800 and 1500 meters. Running in the shorter race, down the backstretch of the last lap I made my move as I had so many times before. To my surprise, I had no more speed than anyone else in the race. I felt the same, but was simply not as fast as before; they stayed with me with apparent ease. As we went through the final curve, I knew I had nothing. Suddenly it all seemed so hopeless—all the work disappearing down the drain. I was tired, had no depth, hadn't been able to sustain my training, and knew I just wasn't the same runner as before.

In a rash moment of irritation, I gave up, slowed down, jogged across the finish line, picked up my sweats, and hastened to the dressing room without a word to anyone. My inner frustration was mounting.

By the time of the 1500-meter final, I'd recovered most of my equilibrium. The pace was extremely slow so "oxygen debt" itself was not really a factor during the run, and I had no problem qualifying.

I was exhilarated in making the team and very anxious to get out of there to share my exuberance with Anne. I had prepacked my '64 Plymouth in anticipation of my takeoff. So in a matter of a couple hours, I headed east. It was a solo, nonstop drive to Manhattan, Kansas, in a mere sixteen hours, an average ground speed of ninety miles per hour. Not exactly what you would call clear, mature thinking, but it certainly depicts my eagerness to be with Anne. We spent a few short days together, Anne attending classes while I continued training on the Kansas-State track.

I'd felt all along that a 3:40 would win the 1500 at Mexico. That would have been the mile equivalent of 3:56 or 3:57. I knew I'd be overjoyed to run that fast, especially when I considered my infamous 4:32 at Alamosa the previous summer.

My respect for Kip Keino's profound abilities multiplied with every report I read. He was turning in some fantastic times. I realized the press, in making me the favorite because of sea-level comparisons, had vastly underrated him and his preparation for Mexico. His fitness was, in a word, awesome.

CHAPTER 9

Disappointment at 7,300 Feet

1968 proved to be an Olympic Games of great contrast. Prior to their opening ceremonies, in an article entitled "Games in Trouble," *Sports Illustrated* wrote:

Never has an approaching Olympics been beset by more immediate and potential problems than Mexico City's—altitude, racial and political boycotts, riots, red tape, delays . . . The curtain is going up, perhaps shakily, but up . . . old XIX staggers into the starting blocks as though it had already been through a war, and it is a good bet that it will not reach the closing ceremonies on October 27 without further suffering." [*Sports Illustrated*, September 30, 1968.]

For distance runners the altitude represented a problem. For other performers, however, it was a blessing of good fortune. The thin air had just the opposite effect on the field events and sprints and propelled the victors to incredible performances. In the sprints, U.S. strength was overpowering. Never had there been such a clustering of amazing records. Wyomia Tyus broke the women's 100-meter record in 11.0. Jim Hines equaled the men's in 9.9. Tommie Smith smashed the 200-meter world record in a run of 19.8. Lee Evans ran an unbelievable 43.8 400 meters. Al Oerter won his fourth gold medal with soaring discus throws. Bob Seagren sailed over 17'8 ½"—a world record. Dick Fosbury created a high-jumping sensation by flopping over the bar backwards at a dizzying 7'4 ½". Most unbelievable of all was Bob Beamon's long jump of 29'2 ½", as if there never was a 28' barrier to bother about (no one had ever jumped over 27'5" before). All in all, in *every single* men's track event under 5000 meters and in *every single* field event, new Olympic records were set. Nine of these were world marks. The women set six track-and-field world records. The thin air, it seemed, would make this one of the most memorable Olympics in history. Maybe all the disquieting talk *had* been a myth.

But as soon as the distance events began, the jubilation turned to dismay. Ron Clarke, who had set seventeen world records and dominated the distance events for years, was easily the odds-on favorite to win the 10,000 meters, if not both the 5000 and 10,000. At one time holder of every world record between two and ten miles, a phenomenal feat not equaled before or since, Clarke was fit and confident of victory and was running well in the 10,000 in what seemed a slow pace. At three laps to go his legs began to deaden, followed by his arms, and then his vision blurred. He hung on desperately, barely staggering across the finish line in sixth place. He collapsed immediately on the infield grass and doctors rushed up to him to administer oxygen while Australians—weeping—clustered about. He lay comatose, seemingly on the verge of death, for over ten minutes. An anxious world watched in somber silence as he gradually came around and was then taken to a hospital. Most physicians and reporters expected him to die that night, but he recovered and, unbelievably, ran in the 5000 meters later in the Games. As the week progressed it became clear that Ron Clarke's collapse was but the tip of the iceberg.

Writing in *Sports Illustrated* just a month later, Dr. Roger Bannister was livid:

> In twenty years of watching athletes I've only once seen a more harrowing sight than Clarke's collapse. . . . That he and many others should have been put in this ridiculous position leaves me frothing with anger. The truth about Mexico's altitude hurt Clarke and twenty more runners in the first few days of the Games—and then I lost count of the number of collapses . . . there were also eighty collapses in the first two days of the rowing. . . .
>
> Doubtless the International Olympic Committee halfheartedly queried the Mexicans on the suitability of the site, but they should have known that Mexican pride made all discussions of risk impossible. . . . The real fault lay with the IOC . . .
>
> The effects of altitude on distance runners are quite simple . . . Altitude can never be "beaten." . . . Clarke's collapse at the end of the 10,000 meters had all the features of circulatory failure. He was ashen and did not recover normal consciousness until he had been given oxygen to breathe for ten minutes. Maurise Heriott, who won a silver medal in the steeplechase at

the Tokyo Olympics, did not recover normal consciousness until two hours after his race in Mexico. Then he said, "All I can remember of the last four laps is vaguely seeing some black spots on the hurdles." He had waited four years since Tokyo for this mockery of a second chance.

By contrast, the steeplechase winner was a tall rather ungainly Kenyan, Amos Biwott, who ran his first steeplechase race a year ago and still leaps the hurdles like a farmer jumping a gate. I am really in favor of Kenya winning as many medals as she can, and Biwott will in time become a great steeplechaser. I simply want to make it clear that a novice won an Olympic title because of the chance of his birthplace. I think this is utterly wrong. [*Sports Illustrated,* November 11, 1968]

The final tabulated results showed that in the five distance events, out of fifteen medals awarded, ten went to altitude-born or -trained Africans. The times were far off what could be considered world class: 14:05 won the 5000, 29:27 the 10,000, 8:51 the steeplechase, and 2:20 the marathon. Both the silver and bronze medalists in the marathon came in just under 2 hours 24 minutes.

Naturally my apprehension grew after Clarke's collapse. Since the 1500-meter final came late on the schedule, the press watched my every move. Everywhere I went someone was waiting to drill me: "What do you think of your chances for the gold?"

I tried to put it out of my mind, but of course that was impossible. Anne and I, along with both our families, went sightseeing, but always there were the reporters, the cameras, the questions.

After one particularly stressful morning, Anne and I climbed the stairs to my Olympic dorm room. She immediately fell in a heap on the couch, but I was too keyed up to sit. I paced back and forth in the tiny room, looked out the window, then turned and started pacing again.

"If I get asked one more question about the altitude or Keino," I finally exploded in frustration, "I think I may deck the guy asking it!"

Anne gave me her most understanding look but said nothing.

"I mean, who do they think I am that I can take all this pressure they keep putting on me? I'm only human, you know!"

"I know," said Anne. "They don't know what they're doing."

"Well they ought to!"

I was really angry. Here I was, finally having the opportunity to compete in another Olympics, and I couldn't even go to the bathroom without someone wanting an interview about it.

"There are limits," I went on, "and I've about reached mine. I mean, gimme a break, guys!"

"It's all right, Jim," said Anne. "They're just interested in you, that's all."

"They're only interested if I win. If I lose, forget it!"

"What do you care what they think? We have each other. Your personhood isn't based on whether you win or lose, what the press says, or what people think."

"But don't you see? I'm trapped. I have no personhood outside of running, according to the press at least. I am Jim Ryun, the *runner.* That's all there is. That's who I am! I hate it! Why can't I just be *me?* Why can't they judge my life and character and personality and worth by who I am? But no, it's only this one race that counts, this one race. I'm just their little puppet. They want to wind me up and see me go out and win and set world records so they'll feel good. But what's going on inside of me—who cares?"

"I care, Jim."

"I know, Anne. I know. But . . . I'm so frustrated. I'm in a box and there's no way out—except to win. And, Lord, I'm so afraid of losing! I'll be judged a failure for the rest of my life. I just don't know if I can take that."

"We'll make it, Jim. We'll make it—together.

She stopped, then changed her tone to one of great intensity. "Look, Jim," she went on, "we're here. You are as ready as you can be. Just go out and do your best. That's all anyone can expect. I love you. And I'm proud of you already. There's nothing you have to prove to me. If you stumble at the starting line and get last, I'm behind you 100 percent and will love you just as much."

"I know you're right," I replied. "I know it . . . in my head. But emotionally it can't help but get to me. I have feelings too. I'm no superhero. I'm just an ordinary guy. Why can't they leave me alone?"

"I know," Anne reassured. "Just remember, I'm with you."

"And these stupid rooms," I went on, unable to stop the torrent once the floodgates of my emotions had been let loose. "These are the worst accommodations I've ever seen. Tiny little rooms, no ventilation . . . and look at that mosquito. It's huge! You'd think they could at least give us rooms where we wouldn't get eaten alive. Hey, throw me that towel."

Anne tossed me one of the towels laying on a table near her. I

Anne and I in Mexico City.

rolled it up, crept stealthily toward the mosquito I had seen, and swatted him dead center.

"Bull's eye!" I shouted.

"Look what you did to the wall," said Anne laughing.

A splotch of red blood dotted the final resting place of the former insect.

"That was a big sucker!" I said.

"There's another one, behind you."

I turned, took aim, and *wham!*—another Mexican monster bit the dust.

"Hey, this is all right!" I said. "We'll get rid of these buggers one way or another." *Bam!* My towel struck home again—three down!

By this time Anne had run into the bathroom, came out brandishing a towel of her own, and a full-scale war was on—two humans against an entire battalion of gargantuan Mexican mosquitoes.

Ten minutes later the mighty Mexican army had fallen, Anne and I lay on the couch laughing uncontrollably, and the formerly stark white walls were speckled from ceiling to floor with huge blots of fresh blood from the defeated foe.

"Look," I said to Anne. "They're going to think some murderous orgy took place in here!"

Anne was laughing too hard to reply.

The anxiety of anticipation continued to build. Three days later

another eruption took place that showed how desperately the volcano rumbling inside me was looking for an excuse to escape to the
surface. Any little thing would do; if my emotions could discover
a pressure valve, they would explode, often unpredictably.

Anne had come over to my room and we were getting ready to
go out to eat. I was in the bathroom shaving. This time, however,
it wasn't mosquitoes. I don't remember quite how it began or who
threw down the first challenge. But suddenly we were embroiled in
the most vicious shaving-cream fight imaginable. It was all over—
in our hair, on our clothes, and all about our faces. What a mess!

But worst of all was the pain in my side from laughing so hard.
Maybe the race would be a bear, but I can tell you it was some time
before I caught my breath after that little fracas. Needless to say,
it was some time before we actually got around to eating that meal.

Qualification had been relatively easy. When Keino and I glided
in one-two in an early heat, it made big news despite the slow time.
"See . . . no altitude problem. Ryun handled him with ease."

Then came the final.

For over a year Jack had tirelessly drilled into me, "Don't run
too fast too soon. A sub-60 quarter is normal at sea level. But at
altitude, a 58 or 59 quarter will put you into such serious oxygen
debt that you'll never recover. There's less oxygen up there and if
you dip into your reserves too early, you'll never get it back . . .
you're finished."

"There's only one chance you have, Jim," he'd said. "Run slow
enough not to get into the sort of problems Clarke had."

How I prayed for a slow pace!

Unfortunately, Keino and his coach realized all this too and put
together a brilliant tactical plan, which they carried out to perfection. As the gun sounded, Keino's Kenyan teammate Ben Jipcho
took off like a jackrabbit and led through the first quarter in an
astonishing 56 seconds. I was in last place and still far faster than
I'd wanted to be—60 seconds. The Kenyans ran a masterful strategi-
cal race. Jipcho and Keino poured it on and, followed by the other
contenders Bodo Tummler and Harold Norpoth, opened a sizable
lead that divided the race into two separate packs. By the 800
meters mark Keino led his group (in 1:55!) and I had moved to the
lead of the other, some forty yards back.

In the third lap Keino accelerated, leaving Jipcho and Tummler behind. I saw the race was in danger of getting away from me and realized that, oxygen debt or not, I had to do something quick. It was a faster pace than I'd planned to run, but it was now or never.

I moved out into the no-man's-land between the two packs for a while. The pace was taking its toll and both groups began to string out. Running hard, I made up the ground quickly, bearing down on the leaders who had amassed such an early margin. I passed the struggling Jipcho, who had spent himself on Keino's behalf, and was by now feeling exhausted myself. But the race was far from over.

At the bell Keino was 2:53—a searing, phenomenal time, an unbelievable *five seconds* ahead of my own world-record-mile pace! Down the backstretch I pressed my tired body for anything it could give me, passing a fading Norpoth and then finally Tummler going into the final turn. I'd done this same thing so many times before. The final straight was my bread and butter, a scorching kick my trademark. But this was no ordinary race. I had the illusion of moving in slow motion. My thighs felt like they had fifty-pound weights attached to them, my lungs were stabbed through with intense, racking agony, reminiscent of Moccasin Pass. The exuberant high of a finishing sprint was nowhere to be found.

How hard it had been to hang back early when my competitive instincts wanted to be up in the thick of battle. Even as I ran I could hear Jack's words ringing in my ears: "Put men on a track at altitude and call out a slow quarter and someone will push the panic button and spurt to the lead. But a crazy fool who doesn't respect the altitude will die. Don't worry what anyone else does, Jim, run *your* race!"

When I passed Norpoth and Tummler there was none of the usual fight left in them. They'd gone into "debt" and had overdrawn their accounts, as Jack was so fond of putting it. Their ashen faces told the story. I lamented their plight, but had other things on my mind.

Keino was too far ahead. Though I was running the final 400 in around 54 seconds, I felt like an elephant plodding around the track. Never had a race been so excruciating! I looked up the long, final straightaway and Keino was still 20 yards ahead. He had run the race of his life. For Jim Ryun a gold medal would have to wait another four years.

1. Kip Keino   3:34.9
2. Jim Ryun   3:37.8
3. Bodo Tummler   3:39.0
4. Harold Norpoth   3:42.5
5. John Whetton   3:43.8
6. Jacques Boxberger   3:46.6
7. Henryk Szordykowski   3:46.6
8. Josef Odlozil   3:48.6
9. Tom Von Ruden   3:49.2
10. Ben Jipcho   3:51.2
11. Andre De Hertoghe   3:53.6
12. Marty Liquori   4:18.2

I staggered up the steep ramp out of the stadium, barely able to walk. In the tunnel I spotted a folding wooden chair. I don't know what it was doing there or why at that particular moment it was unoccupied, but I wasn't about to ask any questions. They shooed you in and out of the stadium rapidly and didn't like dillydalliers. But man . . . I had to have a rest!

"I'll just sit down for a second or two, just to catch my breath," I thought, as I collapsed in the chair.

If I thought that was going to help me catch my breath, I had the proverbial "another thing coming." What a mistake! Not only was I still unable to breath, now I couldn't stand up either. I tried to get moving again a few minutes later and I mean I could not make my legs function. I just kept sitting there, helpless, in that chair. Officials were coming and going, and I desperately tried to make it clear that I needed some oxygen badly, but all my gestures and my foreign tongue could not seem to get through. Jack's prophecy about a knife in my gut could not have been more accurate. All I could think, all I could say was, "Oh God . . . it hurts!"

Keino's run of 3:34.9 has to be one of the outstanding Olympic performances of all time. To have beaten him, even at sea level, would have required a world-record effort. Naturally I was disappointed not to win. But as I have in later years reflected on Keino's achievement, I must simply say that my hat's off to what he pulled off in Mexico. It was one of those exceptional moments when a man's physical conditioning peaks ideally and combines with the perfect jelling of conditions, competition, and pace to produce the kind of performance the world witnesses but once or twice in a

The agonizing second-place finish of the Mexico City 1500 meter. Bodo Tummler is just behind me.

The moment the race was over I struggled to keep my balance.

decade. Such is, I believe, the stature of Keino's accomplishment. He ran a consummate race!

Though Kip Keino has always been considered, in a sense, my nemesis, I feel I must say a word about his most exceptional career, a career that I consider in certain respects has been underrated. Kip Keino was a remarkably versatile athlete. He ran in three Olympiads—1964, 1968, and 1972—in a phenomenal total of seven separate distance races. He won two gold medals and two silver. Though Keino's preference and strength may have been the longer middle-distance events, his record over 1500 meters and the mile is one I consider positively amazing. Back in the days when a four-minute mile was still considered something of a novelty, track buffs used to keep records of who had run how many sub-four miles. Herb Elliott in his brief career ran seventeen. Then in the sixties Jim Grelle accumulated over twenty, and I followed him with twenty-five or thirty. But then Keino came along and ran over fifty! And that's not including equivalent 1500-meter races. In addition, many

The pressure of the Games was visible on both our faces.

of those were hard-fought runs. Keino never liked to sit on a pace and probably ran more fast middle laps than anyone. He came by in 2:55 many times, once in 2:53. That takes guts! The quality, consistency, and longevity of his career certainly places it alongside anyone's.

After I'd begun to recover somewhat, Jack came around.

"Well, doggone," he said, "it sure was faster than 3:40!"

"Just a little," I said, trying to smile.

"You ran a brilliant race, Jim, just like we planned."

"I know," I said. "I'm pleased. I didn't have another tenth of a second in me."

"I tell you," Jack said, "you ran a flawless tactical race. Keino did what he had to do; you did what you had to do. You both got everything out of your bodies they had. And you got one-two. Goodness, Jim, you ran equal to a 3:54—I had no idea you'd do so well!"

"You're right," I said. "And I am pleased. A few months ago it didn't look like I'd be here at all. To run a 3:37.8 and get the silver . . . yeah, the gold would have been nice, but I'm happy with the way it turned out."

"You should be. Like I said, you ran a good race. If you'd tried to go out with Keino, you could easily have wound up dying back in fifth or sixth. Not everyone's been as fortunate as you. Bacheler's in the hospital from the infection going on around here. Bell was favored to win and got cramps from it. You're lucky, Jim. You did great!"

CHAPTER 10

Aftermath of the Silver

Naturally, I knew the public would have preferred a first to a second place. So would I. But I was quite unprepared for the intensity of adverse feelings directed against my performance. Returning from Tokyo, where I'd done miserably, I'd been treated like a hero. All things considered about Mexico City, I was proud of myself. Returning to Kansas, I found everything had changed. Every interview, every question, every article focused on my loss, America's tarnished prestige, my faltering career. The headlines in papers and sports magazines told it all:

> "Will Ryun Be Able to Come Back?"
> "The Truth Behind Ryun's Stinging Defeat"
> "Keino—New King of the World's Milers"
> "What Is Slowing Down America's Fastest Runner?"
> "Is Jim Ryun Past His Peak?"

Phone calls and letters accusing me of buckling under to the pressure became routine. Usually they were unsigned and terse—I'd let America down. I was washed up, a failure! A tougher psychological constitution might have been able to withstand such criticism. At that particular time in my life, considering what I'd been through gearing up for Mexico City, I couldn't.

The upshot was that it became increasingly difficult for me to maintain a sense of personal dignity and worth when all day long I was bombarded with people—even very well-meaning people trying to be sympathetic—implying by their long, dour faces that I had blown it. Daily I saw articles and clippings dissecting and interpreting my 1500-meter "failure" to win the gold medal. The cloud of Mexico hung over me like a mist, driving into my subconscious the inescapable message that I hadn't measured up.

There's an oft-quoted truism that goes "Success is 2 percent perspiration and 98 percent inspiration." In my early years, I simply trained hard, walked out onto the track, ran as fast as I could, and some amazing things happened. People believed in me, few demands were placed on me. No one cared if I won or lost because if I lost, another opportunity would come. The physical and mental were in tune. Therefore, I usually operated close to 100 percent and thus had some good years and great races.

Now suddenly the mental side of Jim Ryun was in disarray and subject to all manner of psychoanalytic speculation.

In one sense, anyone in the public spotlight has to get used to these kinds of tensions. But I *wasn't* used to it, nor could I turn a deaf ear to it as I should have done. Before long my 98 percent "inspiration" was completely gone. I was running on an empty tank—2 percent perspiration.

"Leave me alone," I wanted to shout. "Do you have to add to the burden with your reruns of the film clip and with your analysis of what the future holds for the 'once great' Jim Ryun? Give me a break. Don't you care that I practically spilled my guts out on that track, that I ran as well as was humanly possible for me?"

I should have stopped, taken six months off, and then eased back into running gradually, but this was my senior year. I had to compete one more season to fulfill my scholarship obligations. So I continued to run while not enjoying it. I was determined to gut it out even though I was going through the motions mechanically.

Running was laborious, school difficult, interviews artificial. Kansas had a shot at the NCAA track title in the spring of 1969, creating a new pressure. Everyone was depending on me. If it wasn't the Olympics, it was the NCAA. I *had* to run . . . I had to win! I wanted to do well for Kansas and Coach Timmons, but I also wanted to rest.

Anne remained the only bright spot. No longer was running my whole life. Now my relationship with her had replaced track as my primary reason for being and I was no longer willing to sacrifice everything for running.

We married in January of 1969. The following months were strenuous. She was still in school eighty miles from Lawrence and we managed to see one another only on the rare weekends when I wasn't traveling to compete. It was hardly the best way to kick off a marriage. Anne had remained largely naive about the consuming intensity of competition. It never dawned on her what she'd gotten

Our wedding . . . January 25, 1969.

herself into, until it was too late. As far as she'd been concerned, our relationship had been mostly fun and games. My track life hadn't come into it that extensively.

After she graduated, Anne found herself immediately thrust into a situation in which great expectations were placed on her. Suddenly there were photographers and interviewers after her, for here was a whole new publicity angle. Jim Ryun, after all, had been kind of a dud. A fast runner, no doubt, but you couldn't get him to say much in an interview. But this new wife of his—now she's really something! She'll open right up and talk to you about anything.

Now when the phone would ring, half the time it was for Anne.

"Mrs. Ryun?" the voice on the other end would say.

"Yes."

"I was wondering if you were going to be home tomorrow morning?"

"Well . . . I think so. I mean I have to go out sometime—"

"I'm doing a little article for the newspaper, and I just wanted to know if you'd mind if I came by and asked you a couple of questions; shouldn't take more than five minutes."

"I suppose that'd be okay," said Anne.

"Great. I'll see you around ten."

So when the next morning arrived, up drove not just one person, but two. While the interviewer plied Anne with questions, the other snapped picture after picture, walking around our house, zeroing in on Anne as she talked.

Now Anne is a very good-natured person, but like any woman —especially a young wife—she took certain pride in both her own appearance and that of her home. Trying to smile, put on a cheerful face, and answer the questions graciously for my benefit, out of the corner of her eye she was watching the photographer, wondering what room he was going to discover next.

Then a week later she opened the newspaper to find, not a "little" article at all, but a full three-quarter-page spread featuring all the details of her daily routine, a picture of her standing over the kitchen stove, with a reportorial analysis of *her* thoughts and motives and feelings. Now she was being scrutinized as well.

We were a newly married couple trying desperately to survive the normal adjustments and universal pressures of living together for the first time. Simultaneously we faced the unending stress of being in the national limelight. Anne was cast into a world she scarcely knew existed. I remained in low spirits about the running side of my life.

It grew increasingly clear that my competitive performances were linked to the internal stress operating on me. My body was in tune, but the racing season revealed the strain of the pressure cooker we were in. One minute I would shine, another I'd be a dismal flop. The former Mr. Consistent was up and down.

Anne accompanied me to the Compton Meet at the end of the school year. We had fun together and for a few brief days the pressure was off, but the day prior to the race illustrated Anne's predicament.

She'd been excited about the trip to Los Angeles—we'd go to Disneyland, Knotts, see the ocean, maybe Hollywood. We'd have the time of our lives!

So there we were sitting around the motel room and she was ready to go.

"Hey, let's go out. Sights, shopping. Let's see LA!"

I was lying on my bed not saying a word, flipping casually through a magazine.

"Jim, let's go do something," she insisted.

"Anne, you don't understand," I replied. "The day before a race I rest, sit around . . . and sleep. I have to relax, concentrate, get myself mentally prepared."

This was part of the Jim Ryun package she hadn't foreseen. Not exactly her idea of a great time—being cooped up inside all day.

When the NCAA finals came at the end of June, there it was again, a media blitz. Kansas would be close to the team title. For us to stand a chance I had to win. But Liquori—the kid from New Jersey now running for Villanova—had been close on my heels indoors. He was on his way up, just where I had been several years earlier, hungry for me as I had been for Snell.

The press discussed every detail; all the tiny tidbits of prerace analysis were aired and rehashed. The brash, outspoken kid from the East versus the soft-spoken, one-time king from the Midwest —it was a natural and they milked it for all they could get. Could I hold him off? Was my confidence still shattered? Microphones and flashbulbs were thrust in my face wherever I turned. Was the Ryun era over? Had marriage slowed me down? Had I overcome the "loser syndrome" of Mexico? They quizzed Marty—he spoke with confidence.

"What did I think of him?" they asked.

"He's a great runner," I said, avoiding specifics.

I wasn't prepared for battle. Part of me desired to win, of course. I wanted the team title for Timmie, but another part didn't care in the least if I won. I just couldn't muster the enthusiasm for it any longer. The pressure from the media only sapped my motivation that much more.

Marty thrashed me in the mile by a second and a half—his winning time was 3:57.7; he was running well. It was my first mile loss in four years and would certainly not be my last. We missed the team title by just a few points.

I'd burned myself out; the competitive edge was gone.

I'd wanted to take Anne to Europe. To make it possible, I agreed to run several races there. The trip was all arranged; it would signal the end of my college career, the beginning of a new life with Anne, and would provide us both a much-needed break from the monotony. We looked forward to it. If I could just hold on till then without snapping.

I felt like calling a gigantic press conference, standing up, and shouting: "What can I do to get through to you guys? I've cooperated with you in the past, always given interviews. But can't you see that now I'm trying to establish some sort of normal existence? Don't you care about Anne and me as flesh-and-blood human beings rather than merely the objects of your news stories and photo essays and editorials? Don't we have the right to live without intrusions? Don't you care that my sanity is being destroyed from your constant badgering, wondering what I had for breakfast last Tuesday or what workout I did a year ago last Friday? Can't you . . . can't you lay off and let us be?"

But of course I called no such press conference. Whenever I had the opportunity, I tried to make my voice heard. But there wasn't much "news" in what I was going through personally. That was, after all, the only thing that really mattered—what "news" was there to report about the running exploits of Jim Ryun. No one was listening to what I was trying to say or what was really going on inside of me.

Well, forget it, I thought. I don't owe anyone a thing. I'm under no obligation to grant interviews or dish out nicely phrased answers. And I certainly don't owe the press my marriage and my soul!

"I've had it." I said to myself. "I can't take it anymore. I'm worn out!"

The major portion of the problem was mine. The press was not to blame but merely served as the catalyst bringing my own frustrations to a head. I was unable to confidently say, "Hey, guys, I'm tired and I need a break. No more interviews. Stop coming around the house bugging my wife and quit asking me about running." Instead I glossed over my personal frustrations and reverted, it seemed, to the same old sports jargon about being "a little stale," and "it'll just take some time."

Inside me a silent volcano was bubbling, ready to erupt.

"Jim, honey," Anne said one evening after I got home from a workout, "what's wrong? You seem so tense."

"Nothing," I muttered.

Anne knew me better than that by now. No way was she going to buy that.

"Rough workout today?"

"No . . . the workout was okay."

"Something between you and Timmie?"

"No," I snapped. "Nothing!"

"You're worried about the money, aren't you?" she asked. "Don't worry. It's a tight month, but we'll make it. I had a bunch of coupons, and when I went shopping today the groceries only came to—"

"No, Annie, it's not the money." I said. "Well, maybe that's part of it," I went on. "It's . . . it's *everything!* It's not having any money.

It's training so hard but feeling like a machine and turning in crummy times. It's that guy who's been after me for an interview with *the new married* Jim Ryun. It's trying to—"

I stopped, turned away momentarily, and hid my face with my hands. Anne and I were close, but I wasn't quite ready to let her see tears.

She walked over and put her hand on my shoulder.

"It's okay, Jim. The season's almost over. Then you can relax. No more running for a while. You'll be free from the pressure."

"But that's just it," I said at last, with a shaky voice. "I don't know if I can make it to the end of the season. Every time I even walk to the track, I tense up. I'm just a bundle of nerves. Every day I don't think I can make it another twenty-four hours in this one-dimensional runner's box everyone has me in. I tell you, I'm about to crack!"

Anne said nothing, just stood stroking my back. You see, we really had no one to turn to. We didn't know we could turn to God for help.

And there I'd be the next day, back out on the track, bottling up my inner emotions, gritting my teeth, grinding out the workout, letting no one inside. It was only a matter of time before the lid blew.

That day finally came on the afternoon of the National AAU Track and Field Finals in Miami. It had only been two weeks after the NCAA defeat and the press had blown the race into epic proportions—the rematch between Ryun and Liquori. At this same AAU meet two years ago, I'd set a world record while Liquori, back in the pack, broke four minutes for the first time. Now here we were again, under dramatically altered circumstances. Was this the race between the king and the heir apparent?

I did not care a thing about remaining king. I was concerned with only one thing—getting off the track once my obligations were over with. I would gladly have handed Marty the crown at the starting line if I could have gotten out of the race.

But I toed the line. The gun went off, and away we went.

The first 440 was routine, but I was hardly thinking about the race. I was living in two worlds. My legs were striding along, but my thoughts were a thousand miles away. All the frustrations and conflicting priorities swirled inside my brain as I groped for some

In despair I stepped off the track, tired of the rat race running had become.

After the race I sat and contemplated what I had done.

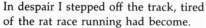

order in the midst of the chaos. It was one of those slices of time when they say "your life flashes before you in a moment." Something like that happened as I ran. All the ups and downs . . . the successes . . . the awards . . . the frustrations . . . my present boredom . . .

Suddenly Anne flashed before my eyes. I was giving her nothing as a husband. She was confused about having to vie for my time and emotions. I loved her more than anything in the world yet was too gutless to make a stand and tell the world. I had vainly tried to express my thoughts but apparently hadn't said it clearly or forcefully enough, because no one seemed to hear. Here I was again— in a race I didn't want to be in, gutting it out as I had so many times this year already, indifferent in spirit about the outcome.

"How much can a guy give?" I said to myself.

I needed a break. Yet I hadn't discovered any way to get one up till then. Around and around the oval treadmill I ran . . . because that was what everyone expected of me. Because I was Jim Ryun.

"Well . . . I'll make a break of my own!"

I can't even say I "decided" to do anything. It all happened so fast. It was a rash and impulsive response. No one had been listening to my pleas, and I knew this would get their attention. At about the 660 mark I simply had had enough.

I stepped off the track and quit the race!

Within a week we'd canceled the European trip, and I didn't run again for a year.

CHAPTER 11

No Solution

If I thought quitting in the middle of the national championships was going to gain any sympathy, I was altogether wrong. As if Mexico City hadn't been enough, now I had *really* added fuel to the burn-Jim-Ryun-in-effigy fire. I'd been outrun, outkicked, hadn't set a world record in two years, had quit in the middle of an important race, and now had publicly announced my retirement from running.

Jim Ryun was through!

I didn't care. Even the postcards I received in the mail simply saying "Quitter!" didn't shake my resolve that I had done the right thing. It was something I needed to do, and the relief was immediate. Looking back, I can see it was probably an immature way of handling the situation, and if it came up now I would most likely respond differently. At the time I felt so stuck between a rock and a hard place that I didn't see any other option open. But still I had no peace within. Both Anne and I were confused as to how to handle life.

The press had a heyday . . . articles poured out. Now that my frustration was public knowledge, the literary investigations began in earnest to explain the reasons and root causes for the demise of my career that had, to all appearances, just ended. This trend continued for a decade, many of the interpretations compassionate and strikingly accurate.

Jim Ryun, the world-record holder . . . the boy wonder, the disappointing silver medalist . . . the troubled young man . . . abruptly stepped off the track in midrace at the National AAU in Miami . . . and, as far as most people could tell, off the edge of the earth as well. [*Sports Illustrated,* November 1970]

There was a time . . . when Jim Ryun could not be beaten. In every race he entered . . . the only question was: Will he set a new world record? Then in 1968 . . . Jim placed second to Kenya's Kip Keino . . . from that time on his running career started to go downhill.

For one thing, Jim suddenly found the demands and pressures of being the nation's track hero greater than the satisfaction . . . He was badgered by press and by track fans to succeed, to explain his success, to be a star —and not let them down. [*Redbook,* July 1972]

Shy and introspective, Ryun brooded about the fragility of his fame. The pleasure he took in the personal challenge of running became strained by the pressures to stay on top. . . . in the 1500 meter . . . Ryun was undone. The silver medalist suffered two more defeats . . . In the second meet, he gave up midway and retired from competition and the harsh glare of publicity . . .

Ryun ran a number of good races, but attention seemed to focus on the heartbreaking ones. He was called erratic and starcrossed. . . . [*Champions of American Sport,* 1981]

That Jim Ryun's career is remembered with disappointment is our fault, not his . . . we wrapped [his] story into a convenient package . . . Our softer hearts felt for him. The hard ones filed him away forever as a loser. He had let America down.

. . . years of perspective tells us that Ryun is a symbol not of failure, but of the dark side of America's mania for success.

It's just that his talent promised so much . . . But even then we couldn't understand the terrible toll a runner's pain and sacrifices have on his psyche . . .

By Mexico City he would be unbeatable. But then his ordeal began . . . Ryun finished second . . . a splendid triumph . . .

Not everyone saw it that way . . . 'I don't think I could have run a better race,' he said. 'It was my best and maybe a little more. . . . [*Philadelphia Daily News,* August 31, 1982]

Let them write. Let them speculate to their heart's content. Let them dissect the Jim Ryun ego and soul and intellect all they wanted. For once I wasn't listening. I was out of competition, no longer making news, and I felt terrific. I thought that, without running, the peace I longed for would come.

The following year I changed my major from business to photojournalism, Anne taught school, and though the workload was

Our inquisitive daughter, Heather checking
out one of Daddy's trophies.

heavy, I was ready to graduate in 1970. Anne and I spent time that
year doing things we'd never been able to squeeze in before. We
made new friends, played tennis and racketball, refinished furniture. We both gained considerable weight, she from being pregnant.
I quickly ballooned up over 200 pounds. Our relationship was
sound and we grew to love one another even more. My only regret
about what I'd done in Miami was that I hadn't had the courage to
take action sooner.

We continued to live in Lawrence where I could hardly help but
remain a well-known object of interest. To a certain extent, therefore, the publicity surrounding our lives kept up. It was easier to
handle now because I was asked questions about our marriage, my
photography, other interests, and not exclusively about running.
When pictures appeared in the paper, Anne and I were both included, perhaps riding bikes or walking together. I was shown in

The whole family.

street clothes, not running trunks. Thus in the midst of ongoing media exposure, at least there was a degree of normalcy. The pressure of racing was gone. I very much enjoyed that year.

Some time after the Miami race I received a call from Howard Cosell asking me to come to New York for a televised interview to explain the incident and why I had quit the race. At first I refused, certain he would roast me publicly. After considering it further, I changed my mind. He assured me he would allow me the floor without criticism.

When I arrived, Howard rolled out the red-carpet treatment, took me to Club Twenty-One, introduced me around to his friends, treated me with the utmost courtesy, and was very sympathetic toward my whole situation. Following later in the interview, after showing a clip of the race, he was most understanding.

"Jim," he began, "I know of no athlete in this country whose personal and private life has been subject to the scrutiny yours has over the past decade. The number of articles about every phase of your life has been staggering. And especially when you consider your age when it all began. You were probably this country's most public teenager during the '6os. There had to have been enormous pressure on you."

"I have a tendency to forget what those early years were like," I responded. "It's something you get used to in a way, having someone probe into some corner of your life whenever you turn around. But, yes . . . it never goes away and eventually wears you down."

"And is that what was going through your mind in the race we just saw?"

"I would have to say so. I just needed a chance to get out from under all that for a time. You can't imagine what it's like trying to establish a marriage under those conditions."

"Do you still feel good about what you did?" he asked.

"Yes . . . I guess I do. It could well be that in the frustration I overreacted to the stresses. But I had to do something."

"I understand you received some pretty nasty mail after the episode?"

"That's true," I said. "It wasn't too pleasant. But on the other side, there have been an equal number of very positive and encouraging letters and articles, supportive and sympathetic. Joe Garagiola wrote me. So did a judge in Philadelphia, a priest in Oregon. Other people I didn't even know."

I then went on to honestly express many of the feelings I'd had about the pressures and stresses of being in the public eye. Howard was completely true to his word—he spoke not a word of criticism. I came away with a great respect for him. It caused me to reflect on some of the positive influences of the media and the close bonds with other press men and women I'd developed. Rich Clarkson, who'd taken more pictures of me than anyone, and I had become very good friends. Under his guidance I was headed for a career in journalism, as a free-lance sports photographer. I certainly had nothing intrinsically against the media. It was not that I came to blows every time someone wanted to take a picture or interview me. I simply needed time away from that sports-centered environment to solidify my broadening priorities about living.

In 1970 we moved to Topeka where I took a job full time as a photographer with the *Topeka Capital-Journal.* Our daughter Heather

Anne and I with Heather.

was born that June to add another loving spark to our relationship. And I began to notice with some alarm the forty-one pounds I'd put on!

It began again initially from Anne's encouragement.

"When are you going to start back up?" she asked one evening.

"Start up what?" I said.

"Running, silly!" answered Anne laughing.

"I don't know. I hadn't really thought about it."

"You know you want to," she said with a playful twinkle in her eye.

"What makes you say that?"

"I can tell. Your feet are itching to be out there."

"Nah!" I insisted.

"You can't fool me, Jim Ryun!"

"A little jogging wouldn't hurt. Have you taken a look at me lately—I'm a regular balloon."

"I wasn't going to say anything about it," replied Anne with another laugh, "but now that you mention it . . ."

"Trying to set up a little physical fitness program for your tubby hubby," I said, throwing a pillow-cushion at Anne where she sat opposite me, "that was it all along, wasn't it?"

"Now I wouldn't do that. Besides, I put on weight, too."

Anne and I running sprints.

"But you had a good excuse. Pregnant women are *supposed* to get fat."

"Fat? I didn't get *fat*. Just a little . . . well, chubby."

"Well, call it what you will. *I'm* rapidly getting fat!"

"So let's start jogging," suggested Anne. "I'll do it with you. Or I'll bike along and we'll put Heather in a back-carrier. It'll be fun!"

"I don't know. I've enjoyed not running."

"This time it'll be different. It can be a family activity. You can enjoy it. Let's have fun with it!"

And who can deny it—I *do* love to run.

So we started jogging together, very gradually, just to take the weight off. Anne hadn't run before and wanted to take it up to find out what my world had been like. The first time she thought she'd prove to me she could do it and determined to go as far as she could. She made it two miles, and I was proud of her. She then worked up to four miles, and we began to have a lot of fun together, running in the country, talking about the houses we'd pass, doing crazy things along the way like playing tag. When we ran at the track we'd take Heather along and park her in the middle of the infield.

It did not take long for the inevitable to begin to happen. The jogging turned to running, the running to training, and my thoughts

After the San Francisco race, Anne was presented with an
engraved Mother of the Year award by the meet director,
saluting her role in my return to competition.

could not help but be drawn toward Munich, site for the upcoming
1972 Olympics.

   Articles gradually began to appear once more: "Guess Who's
Training Again?" . . . "Who Is the Mysterious Runner on Those
Kansas Roads?" . . . "A Ryun Comeback?" To begin with they were
merely curious, then grew more pointed: "Why are you training, Jim

Ryun? What are you up to? Is the retirement over? Is this a full-scale return to the ring?"

I tried to be casual, but there was no avoiding it. "Yes, I'm going to give it another try."

Before long our marriage and my running were just as exposed to public view as ever. I'd had a break and in that sense was refreshed. Now Anne was fully involved in it with me, and the press at last seemed to accept the partnership aspect with which we now approached running. In fact, there were as many articles about Anne's role encouraging me back into running as there were on me. We put on a cheerful countenance, smiled when the cameras clicked away, and said to everyone who asked, "We're running for fun."

My conditioning improved steadily and I eventually scheduled my first race nineteen months after retirement—an indoor mile at the Cow Palace in San Francisco. I was quite naturally nervous, wondering if I still had it, wondering if the weight gain or layoff would hurt me, wondering if I was still a "psycho." The articles literally poured off the presses about my comeback race, many of which were sent us in the mail. Actually, considering all the hype for the race, it's a wonder I was as relaxed as I was.

The race felt great:

For Jim Ryun it has begun again. Nearly nineteen months have passed since he stepped off the track in Miami and into a self-imposed exile—and then suddenly, last week in San Francisco, it was as if he had never been away. For there he was, on the track at the Cow Palace, in the familiar pink and blue of the University of Kansas ghosting along in fourth place, and after only two laps of the mile run the old magic was gripping the crowd. . . . [*Sports Illustrated*, February 1, 1971]

I ran the final quarter in 56.5 for a mile in a relatively easy 4:04. It was a weight lifted from my shoulders. I could still run after all! The next time out, in the San Diego Sport Arena, was equally uplifting:

. . . Chuck LaBenz staked his claim to the lead from the gun, blasting the first quarter mile in 54.2. Ryun was forty yards behind at the split, and ten yards back of LaBenz's teammate, John Mason. LaBenz kept the steam up, pulling out yet another ten yards on the steady Kansan. Ryun's steadiness derived from experience. He knew LaBenz couldn't keep up such a hot pace. . . . Tough New Zealander Dick Quax moved past Ryun into third.

Indoors against Sam Bair (number 230) at NCAA Indoor
Championships in Detroit, Mich.

It was actually a perfect Ryun race. He had paced sensibly and still had
a lot left for his devastating, trademark kick in the final quarter—and a
perfect rabbit to chase, in the form of Quax.

Ryun put Quax to sleep with two laps left. He lifted his knees and
rocked his head from side to side and was JIM RYUN. He set after the
leaders like a hungry hound after an old 'coon. Mason took the lead from
LaBenz on the penultimate lap. Bang! the last lap—Ryun snatched the lead
from Mason, hit the tape in 3:56.4, and tied Tom O'Hara's indoor-mile
mark. Jim Ryun was back, people said, but, in truth, he had never been

away. [Krise and Squires, *Fast Tracks* (Lexington, Mass.: S. Greene Press), p. 201]

Later in the spring I ran 3:55 at the Kansas Relays before a stadium full of enthusiastic hometown spectators. My confidence had returned and I felt very pleased with my progress.

One of the difficulties about this period of time was that I was basically training alone. I no longer had Coach Timmons guiding my every step. There was an element missing in not being part of a program someone else had established for you. Anne and I were therefore on the lookout for a situation I could plug into that would provide stability and continuity to my training. In addition, we recognized it was time for a move away from Kansas. I found it difficult to flex my wings as an adult with broadening concerns while I remained under the watchful eye of family and friends. Growing into maturity from adolescence is always difficult, but it was made all the more complex because my youth had been so public. I could never escape being forced into the mold of what I had been. Finding my identity as a man would never come easily at home. I was the "favorite son" of Kansas but I needed to be a man —my *own* man.

For some time we had been discussing a move and talking about possibilities. I was drawn to the West Coast becasue of its weather and because postcollegiate running clubs abounded there. I was sure I would quickly be able to find people to run with who would help me progress. Eugene, Oregon, in particular seemed to suit us, and I had always loved that locale. We continued to discuss a move, gradually decided on Eugene as our future home, and in January of 1971 we packed all our worldly possessions into a U-Haul truck and with our six-month-old baby, struck out for the West to seek our fortune. I was fully optimistic that in the running environment that Eugene had become and with the enthusiastic support of many Eugene citizens, including a job as a company photographer for the Bohemia Lumber Company, I would find the camaraderie and coaching I needed to continue to progress toward peak form.

One thing I hadn't foreseen about Eugene, however, was the pollen problem. My allergies hadn't given me difficulties in Kansas for years, and I never gave them a thought before moving west. My body began to react, causing my lungs and throat passages to swell. Training went tolerably well for a while; it takes some time for the

The dream mile in the Martin Luther King Games. As we circled the track, Marty's strength and determination were evident . . .

. . . as was his jubilation at the finish when he held me off in 3:54.6.

cumulative effect of an allergic reaction to make itself felt. But after a while my performance began noticeably to lag.

I continued to work hard, yet didn't realize how much the pollen was sapping my strength. At the Martin Luther King Games in Philadelphia I was very pleased with a mile in 3:54.8. However, I finished a stride and .2 behind Marty Liquori who had in my absence turned into one of the world's best.

Without realizing it then, a familiar pattern was starting to emerge. The press played up the loser-syndrome angle. In my next race, which was in Eugene, I was beaten badly by Steve Prefontaine. By the time of the AAU finals the following month, my allergies had grown so severe that I was flat on my back in bed.

"When is it going to end?" I thought. "If it's not altitude or mono, it's allergies!" Once again the image of Jim Ryun as over the hill became popular column material, and hints of the same old depression began creeping back. Eugene was definitely not working out as the running utopia we had hoped for.

Maybe I was a psycho after all!

Yet still driving me was that romantic hope that once I finally reached the summit—the victory stand in Munich—lasting fulfillment would be mine.

Now that I was no longer in school, money had become a focal issue. I had a family to support and bills to pay. If I intended to train twice a day, I certainly couldn't work eight hours too. Thus I became inexorably sucked into the dilemma of whether to accept under-the-table cash for racing, which was forbidden by amateur rules and watched very closely by the AAU. Most top athletes (the exceptions were very rare) were paid to enter large meets and were normally left alone by the AAU. But I had always been observed very closely. If I won a TV or radio for a collegiate race (which is common), the NCAA officials were on the phone to Timmie the very next day to insist that my prize be returned. I had many close friends who won literally dozens of such prizes, very costly, who were never asked about their winnings. (Watches were the most common; some guys collected more watches than they had friends to give them to.) Everything I received was turned over to the association.

In 1971, however, it was different. I'd been holding down photographic jobs since graduation and between work, family, and training, I had neither time nor money enough to go around. I'd be up at 5:30—before the sun was up—for a morning workout, then on the job at 7:30 or 8 until late afternoon, and then another workout. It was a demanding schedule. Back at the university, though the stress had been severe, at least my financial life had been much simpler. Not anymore. Money became a constant anxiety.

Therefore, the pressure to compromise my previous values grew keen. I now felt I *had* to have money in order to run. The offers were always there. Many of the guys took it—no big deal. Just a white envelope stuffed with some cash. It happened all the time. I didn't feel "right" about doing it, but it was a matter of survival. We simply couldn't make ends meet. This was one of those instances where it boiled down to a very simple choice: did I want to run, or not? If so, I had to take the money. Since I wanted to run, I began taking the money.

"There's no other way I can keep running," I'd say as Anne and I went round and round trying to decide what to do, taking turns on each side.

"We're desperate."

"But do we *have* to?" she would ask. "Is there any other way?"

"That's one of the realities of athletics in this country," I would go on, trying to justify what I didn't feel comfortable about. "Unless you have some sort of financial backing, you have to. True amateurism is dead. To continue competing you either put enormous burdens on yourself and your family . . . or you cheat. The choice is that simple. If I want to make that Olympic team, we have to take some money for some of these races."

Like many more outspoken track-and-field athletes, the dilemma angered me in a way. If I'd been a professional in any other sport, I wouldn't have had to face it. But though we saw the hypocrisy of the AAU's double standard, we nevertheless remained unsettled about breaking it. We'd both been taught to believe in God and could, therefore, not escape the feeling of doing wrong.

I was uncomfortable to begin living a lie—Mr. All-American Boy dishonestly on the take, glancing around to make sure no one was looking while grabbing an unmarked envelope full of cash. It was an agonizing pass to come to.

When Timmie questioned me about it, I point-blank lied to him: "I am not taking any money." In so doing, I was miserable with myself.

Yet all the while, as I'd seen when a child, crossing into the boundaries of "sin" did not—as I half expected—bring down God's vengeance on us. However, the anxiety we felt far outweighed the peace we so desperately sought. We wanted someone to turn to but felt no one really understood. It was probably as a result of this crossroads that our real search for God began.

After all this soul-searching, I only ran three races for money— just enough to help us past a rough time. By today's standards for world-class athletes, the paltry amounts seem laughable. But for us, back then, it was quite a step to take.

Following the pollen-polluted spring of 1971, I'd been scheduled to run a couple races in Europe. By now I was extremely apprehensive about running in a location where I wouldn't be able to breathe. So I questioned the meet promoters very specifically about potential pollen difficulties and received the firmest of assurances that I would be completely free of any problems. So Anne, Heather, and I packed our bags and flew off for Europe.

In Stockholm I'd been entered in an "Olympic Rematch" against Kip Keino. There I was once more, my entire career on the line.

Although I was deeply motivated to win that race, it was a disaster. Keino won easily in a fast 3:54, and I came wheezing along, hardly able to breathe, dead last in 4:17.

CHAPTER 12

Turmoil

In August 1971 we moved to Santa Barbara. I had no job and no prospects, but there were people to train with at Club West and we hoped the change in environment would help the allergies. I landed a job as a line photographer and under the supervision of Dr. Jay Keystone, my breathing began to improve. It had to—the Olympics were approaching.

As soon as Jay began treatment, he wrote the IOC (International Olympic Committee) to make certain all the serums and medications he was using were allowable by IOC regulations. He received an affirmative response.

Santa Barbara represented a very hopeful environment. We enjoyed ourselves there. We made friends and my training once more resumed some regularity. Yet there remained an undercurrent of dissatisfaction brewing beneath the surface of my consciousness. Stepping off the track in Miami had been a concession to my frustrations but not a cure.

Perhaps I never accepted my role as a public figure. It was something I neither sought nor wanted. It just came and then ate away at me. After nine years in the position of always being watched, the stress was inescapable. On the whole, the press had liked me. The real burden was that I couldn't *escape.* I was taking a shower once when I looked down and saw several hands under the stall door seeking autographs. In Tokyo a photographer followed me right into the shower. I've seen published pictures of me eating, tying my shoelaces, studying, yawning, sleeping. It was just the sheer *quantity* of publicity that wore us down, along with the lack of any clear direction in our lives.

Staying with us for a while, a friend with whom we were working on a project walked in from the garage lugging a huge box he could hardly lift by himself. We'd shown him the corner of our storage area where a stack of boxes contained the Ryun archives, and this was the first of what would be a week of pillaging through it for him. Groaning, he inched through the door, dropped the box, and dragged it toward the living room where he overturned the contents on the floor.

"My gosh!" he exclaimed. "This is unbelievable! There must be a thousand different clippings and magazines and pictures here! It'll take me a month just to sort through this one box!"

"It better not!" said Anne playfully. "I never gave you permission to redecorate my living room floor!"

"I'll work late," he replied with a laugh, "but . . . good night! There's just so much—and this only covers a year or two!"

"Annie," I said, "did you show him that scrapbook you made?"

"No. I'll go get it."

Returning a few minutes later, Anne set the former carpet–sample book stuffed with pictures and articles down on the floor in front of our friend. By this time he was thoroughly engrossed in his work and we resumed what we had been doing.

About half an hour later I heard another exclamation and went to investigate.

"I've been looking at this scrapbook," he began. "Do you know that there are 240 articles here covering only eight races during a relatively slow six months?"

"I'd never really stopped to count," I said.

"Don't you realize what that means?" My friend was incredulous. "The volume of publicity is . . . why, it's staggering! Here's one race . . . look—"

I watched as he quickly thumbed through the scrapbook.

"One race! And there are seventy-eight articles here. Seventy-eight! What about those things written that were never sent to you?"

"There were a lot," I admitted.

"Can you imagine, though," he continued. "I mean, over the ten years of your running career . . . well, it boggles the mind to think how much was written."

"I'm glad I never saw the half of it," I said.

"We saw enough," interjected Anne. "Too much! There were times it really seemed like if we so much as walked out of the house we'd see our picture in the paper the next day."

"That's probably an exaggeration," I said. "But Anne's right— it did seem that way. I wearied of it. I just wanted to run, do my best, enjoy my family, and be a regular sort of guy."

Years before, I'd grown irritated at the external annoyance of the publicity. Now, however, I was gradually coming to see that the newsmen and photographers and autograph seekers weren't the prime problem. I couldn't blame them. They were simply doing their jobs and many persons in my shoes were able to handle the notoriety fine. The turbulence of my reaction illustrated my own lack of understanding about the responsibility of being a celebrity. I began to see that I had to stop pointing my finger, as if seeking a scapegoat.

The problem, at its most fundamental level, was *me*—not anyone else. Simply put, much as I might like to avoid admitting it, I wasn't at peace with myself.

I had the deep feeling that there must be more to life than this treadmill I was on. I'd always assumed that if I became a success and achieved great things, the result would be peace inside. There had come fragmentary moments of satisfaction and contentedness. If I ran a particularly good race or set a new record of some kind, certainly there was a gratification that came along with it. Yet usually by the next day whatever temporary peace of mind had accompanied the achievement was gone. In its place was that never-ending sense of unrest, that feeling that I had to keep striving for one more mountaintop of accomplishment. Any lasting peace was never there. Even though I had attained greatness in the world's eyes, when I stopped, stood still, and was willing to look myself straight in the eye, I knew something was missing.

It was this undetermined sense of emptiness that kept us aware of spiritual things. Anne and I continued to attend church somewhat sporadically, but there had never been any crossover into the daily events and emotions of our lives. Church was often routine habit, yet our upbringing made us feel a sense of duty to continue a thin line of allegiance between ourselves and the church.

Shot-putter Neil Steinhauer was one of our closest friends in Eugene. I had known Neil for several years. There was something about him that was really special. Not only was he a world-class athlete, he was so fun-loving, with such a zest for life. I felt good just being in his presence. He had this peculiar habit of talking about religious things in the most everyday situations. "Hey, Jim, let me tell you about a prayer the Lord answered yesterday," he might say, or "I was reading in my Bible this morning and you won't believe the verse I found," or "The Lord's really been leading me to pray for so-and-so,"—who happened to be a competitor of his. He talked about church as if he really enjoyed it.

In fact, Neil had been sending us Christmas cards ever since I'd known him. Always at the bottom was a handwritten notation of a Bible verse. Puzzled at first by them, I thought they were references to his recent shot-putting distances. When Anne and I later realized what the number signified, we thought it a little strange. We had not been taught to take Bible verses that seriously or literally. In fact, we had not been trained to read our Bibles at all!

During our months in Eugene, Anne and I were really sinking, not because of the people there, or the job, but simply because we'd hit a low point emotionally. Thus Neil represented a breath of fresh air in what was a very drab existence. We couldn't help but be a little curious about what set him apart.

Other little "coincidental" occurences gradually began coming our way. A well-known Episcopal priest by the name of Dennis Bennett conducted a special meeting at Anne's folks' church in Ohio that they attended. They bought a copy of his book and then sent it to us. About the same time Anne's sister sent us a copy of the book *God's Smuggler,* the exciting story of Brother Andrew's exploits smuggling Bibles behind the Iron Curtain.

While in Eugene the offer was made to Anne and me to use a small cabin up in the Mackenzie River valley for a few days. It would give us a chance to get away for a while, the allergies could dry up, and it sounded good. We slept in, wore old clothes, relaxed, and had time to talk and do whatever we wanted. What a wonderful respite from the grind it was!

"I didn't know you'd brought those," I said as Anne was unpacking some of our bags. There was *God's Smuggler* and a couple other books on spiritual things.

"Well," she answered, "I thought we might want something to read. We didn't really have anything around the house, so I grabbed them."

Later that afternoon, after looking all about the cabin and familiarizing myself with our new surroundings, I plopped into a chair and began thumbing through *God's Smuggler.*

"Hmmm," I thought to myself, "no pictures. Oh well . . . nothing much else to do." So I started reading casually, just to pass the time.

It was not the sort of book I was in the habit of reading. After I'd left home for the university I'd decided that whatever religion I still possessed as a carry-over from my childhood was doing me no good, so I quit attending church altogether. I didn't alter my lifestyle notably; I simply became uninterested. What was said in church appeared to me phony, unrealistic, and for that matter, so did those attending. After all, here were people who claimed to believe in a life-changing faith but their lives weren't changing! If the words had no meaning and relevance for how life was to be lived, it seemed a total waste of time and energy.

That was still my view, though we continued to attend church from time to time. Long ago I'd stopped attending *my* church, opting to attend Anne's church because I didn't want church affiliation or religion to divide us. The unseen raging of emotions deep inside over the years, because of the turmoil of my life of running, had caused me to question much of what I had previously believed. The result was a silent cynicism toward the whole religious framework of my upbringing. Without such stress there is often no need to search and analyze one's life. Thus I am grateful for this four-year period between 1968 and 1972 when nothing seemed to go right. Without these struggles I might never have paused to ask what life was supposed to be about.

Thinking I would simply read for a few minutes, I still sat reading about Brother Andrew two hours later. It was an incredible story! I am an adventurer at heart, and this story was a breathtaking adventure, one in which God was working through people, to give others hope.

I finished *God's Smuggler* the following day and immediately tackled the next book. Finally my mind was just too full. I put down the book I was reading, rose from my chair, walked outside, and headed along a path from the cabin. I had to be alone. I had to think.

I walked silently through the tall, fragrant groves of pine trees that bordered the Mackenzie River, thoughts tumbling through my brain about what I had been reading. I sensed new dimensions of thought being triggered in areas I had never stopped to consider. Here were people not just *talking* about their faith in God, they were *doing* something. They took prayer and living according to the Bible seriously. Their lives had something special, something different than I'd seen in any church I'd been in. I thought of Neil. Yes, they were like him. Was this what made him so unique? Why, here was Brother Andrew taking his life in his hands, praying that God would temporarily blind the Communist guards from seeing the Bibles jammed into every square inch of his tiny Volkswagen. Why were these Bibles so important? I had a Bible and never read it. Why would people risk their lives to give Bibles away?

These people believed in modern-day miracles, trusted God in seemingly foolhardy ways, and yet were so at peace with themselves. It was new to me—like no form of spirituality I'd heard about in all my years of church attendance.

The common fallacy, when you've been raised in a constricting environment, is to throw off its shackles completely, to rebel against everything your conservative past stood for. For me that would have been too simple. I wanted to find the truth, wherever it was. If there was no truth in Christianity, I wanted nothing to do with it. But if there *was* truth there—no matter that I had been raised in a narrow sect where that truth wasn't understood or practiced—I wanted to find out. I didn't want to be guilty, as so many of my generation have been, of "throwing the baby out with the bathwater." I wanted to find the truth, wherever that search took me.

Insight came to me very slowly. Everything about this "new" brand of spirituality ran counter to what I'd been taught. The religious tenets of the Church of Christ allowed none of this "modern-day miracle" stuff. Even though I had not adhered to those past narrow creeds myself, I still found myself suspicious of these new revolutionary concepts. Maybe, just maybe, I should check out what the Bible had to say. After all, what this book and many others were saying was that Jesus is alive today, that He is still doing miracles; still doing today what He did back in the days of the Bible.

We returned from the cabin to the tedium of my attempt to struggle back to the top of the running world.

Meanwhile the monotony of the daily grind wore down Anne's sensitive emotional nature perhaps more rapidly than it did my more moderate temperament. The move from Kansas to Oregon had uprooted her equilibrium more than either of us realized. Not only was the secure environment of the past gone, but now she faced the stresses of motherhood and being my wife—no easy assignment, but one she did enjoy even if life was a bit unsettling. We had each other and that was all that really mattered.

Externally we appeared a beautiful and happy couple. Internally, we were full of questions. "There has to be more to life than this!" our insides were screaming, but we had no idea even where to begin looking to find it.

While not active in church, we considered ourselves Christians. Well . . . certainly we were Christians; we were raised in America, weren't we, going to Sunday school and learning the right sorts of things? What was happening was that we were learning "head" knowledge, not heart-applied knowledge that would give us tools with which to live. The inner skepticism I felt, to my way of thinking, in no way disqualified me from being a Christian. Anne and I were trained as far as our parents knew to train us and were now doing everything we knew to do.

Time, by its miracle, has a way of burning off detail to reveal with clarity the essential track of life's progress. Looking back on these factors allows us to recognize forces in our lives we were unaware of at the time. I can see why I read those books at the cabin, why we occasionally attended church, and why I trained so hard for Munich. I was searching for meaning, for something to fill the void inside. I was drawn to the life-style I'd read about. Neil and Brother Andrew had . . . something! I didn't know what, but I liked how it looked. We wanted what they had. How were we to get it?

Moving to Santa Barbara from Eugene represented for us the chance to start over. Not only were we very optimistic about the running, but at the same time we hoped to get our lives emotionally back on track as well. We couldn't take the turmoil any longer. We had wandered too long in the maze of the running world. We had no direction, no control, no goals to latch on to.

Therefore we determined, "Okay, in Santa Barbara, we're going to find a church that offers us something." So our first Sunday in Santa Barbara we attended three different Episcopal services, one right after the other. That was how anxious we were to find something to grab hold of. The next week we attended still another—a charismatic Episcopal church.

Were we in for a surprise! At this service all sorts of unusual things were going on. People were singing, laughing, greeting one another with hugs, lifting their hands in the air during the service. Anne and I spent most of the time shooting sidelong glances toward one another as if to say "What have we gotten ourselves into?" The most striking feature of it was that everyone seemed to be having so much fun. No down-in-the-dumps, dull spiritual doldrums here. Man, these people were having a ball!

Everyone was so friendly. You couldn't help but have a good time. Once we loosened up a bit, it was the most enjoyable church service I'd ever attended. Afterwards everyone was milling around, introducing themselves, making us feel right at home. I felt a hand on my shoulder, turned around, and saw Paul Herman, an Olympic decathlete I had met while training at the University of California at Santa Barbara.

"Jim, good to see you. I didn't know you were an Episcopalian."

"Paul," I said, turning around, "It's good to see you! We're trying to find a church and thought we'd try this one."

We chatted awhile. Paul introduced us to his wife, Gwen, and their children.

"We're not meeting at the church next Sunday," Paul said. "We're going to have an outside service followed by a picnic. Could you come?"

I shot Anne an inquisitive glance.

"Sure," replied Anne, "why not?"

"Well, why don't you come by our house first, since you don't know where the park is, and we'll go together."

So a week later we found ourselves following Paul and Gwen to the park for the Sunday service and picnic. And boy, those people just didn't do things the way we'd seen in any Episcopal church we'd ever been in. Worshiping outside really appealed to us, as did the whole special flavor of friendliness, of raising hands, and clapping and singing. They enjoyed it so much! We were intrigued.

At the picnic we met a couple, Susan and Jay, who had a baby daughter born within twenty-four hours of our own Heather. In addition, we just happened to live in an apartment that was across a field from their house. If there's anything young mothers can relate instantly to, it's their children, and Susan and Anne hit it off immediately.

Our curiosity about this fellowship of people was aroused and we found ourselves going back Sunday after Sunday. Being more reticent myself, part of me was still hanging back. Not so with Anne. Here were people enjoying life and she jumped right into the thick of it. She knew they had what she wanted.

It didn't take long before Anne and Susan were seeing one another daily, chatting about the babies, getting together for the two girls to play, shopping, and talking on the phone. They took an evening sewing class together. Susan represented for Anne what Neil had to me—a buoyant, joyful approach to life. She, like him, attributed it to being a Christian. She was happy and full of life, and she said, "My joy comes from my relationship with Jesus."

Before long Susan had invited Anne to an evening Bible study they held in their home every week. A little reluctant to go alone, Anne asked the wife of a fellow runner of mine to accompany her. The whole time, while prayer was going on, the two of them sat there in awe looking around at what was going on while everyone else had their heads bowed and their eyes closed. They couldn't believe their ears! Telling me about it later, Anne's comments seem so humorous now.

"There was even a nurse, Jim," she said, "and she was just praying along with everyone else. And you know nurses, they're pretty smart! There were two guys that work for the government —and high up, too!"

I sat listening, quizzing her on what had happened.

"I mean, these were not stupid people. They really believe in all that stuff. More than that . . . they're Episcopalians. They couldn't have gone too far wrong if they're Episcopalians!"

A real hunger began to develop in Anne to be around these people. We'd never seen anything like this. It was just so intriguing to us, and a real answer to the deep longing we had within us to find peace. Susan's faith excited her, not merely on Sunday, but from Monday through Saturday as well. It found its way into every part of her life. Far from being a drudgery, Susan's spiritual life gave her a radiance and exuberance that we couldn't help but be drawn to.

She would do the oddest things! One evening she and Anne were sitting in the car after returning from their sewing class. They were chatting away, as was their custom, when Anne happened to casually mention that she had a cold sore in her mouth that was really painful and uncomfortable.

"Well, let's just pray for it then," said Susan without a moment's hesitation. Before Anne could utter a word, Susan burst into spontaneous prayer—right in the car!

"Lord, I simply ask you to heal Anne's soreness and take that pain away, in Jesus name. Now I thank you Lord for your answer."

Now that was pretty bizarre behavior!

Anne shifted a little uncomfortably in her seat but said nothing. Susan spoke about God as if He was right beside her and about healing and miracles as if they were commonplace.

It was most intriguing. But Susan wasn't the only one. Everyone in that church spoke the same brand of spiritual lingo and lived the same sort of life-style that we'd seen in Neil Steinhauer and read about at the cabin, not based on church rules or religious doctrine but—as they put it—on a friendship with Jesus. He was not just a man in history, Susan said, but someone whose spirit lives on, someone with whom we can interact in a daily, moment-by-moment way.

Telling me about it later that evening, my initial reaction was, "Yeah . . . that's neat, but, well Susan *is* a little different!"

Yet there was an appeal in her way of life. Not to mention the fact that the next day Anne's cold sore was gone! Now that made us stand up and take notice.

We continued to attend the charismatic Christ the King Episcopal church and continued to be drawn to this life-style so refreshingly different from the humdrum and ordinary. It sounded so appealing—freedom from the frustration and pressure of the world's values.

From so many different directions it suddenly seemed we were being brought face-to-face with Christians whose lives were truly distinctive. Anne was already being drawn into friendship and fellowship with many people and was discovering again the joy of living that had been missing. I continued to stand back, cautious, just observing. Everything these people stood for and all they told us cut across the grain of my upbringing. I was interested, even drawn to what they had to share and intrigued about the newfound priorities I could see in their lives, but I remained reluctant to say much or to commit myself to anything.

I'd read the books, but it had been possible to put them back on the shelf without responding in any way. Suddenly we were face-to-face with friends. We couldn't shelve them away, out of sight. They were breathing, dynamic, living people whose spiritual lives had come alive. Something greater than the church was happening here. We were finally coming to grasp the reality that maybe going to church hadn't made us Christians any more than sitting in a chicken coop would have made us chickens. After a lifetime in and out of churches, we were now seeing what appeared to be the real thing.

The upshot of it all was that I began to get sweaty palms. Whatever was happening in the lives of these "Christians" giving their lives direction was something I knew I badly needed. The moment I realized that, I could foresee that some sort of personal response would ultimately be required of me.

But I was not yet ready to make any pledges. I continued to wait and examine this new phenomenon without saying much one way or the other.

The Olympic year arrived. The allergies were coming under control, or so I thought. My training had been going well, but when it came time to race I found myself flat. After a good start the 1972 season began to go sour and my times became far more erratic than the disaster of a year earlier. At least in 1971 I'd had my allergies to blame. Now, however, there was *no* reason! Was I a psychological basket case . . . mentally burned out . . . ready for a breakdown?

I dropped to a disheartening 4:13 in the *LA Times* Indoor Meet. In anguish afterward I called Timmie on the phone. "What would you think of me coming back to Kansas?" I asked. "Would you take me on again?"

We'd tried Eugene and now Santa Barbara. And though from a personal standpoint, things were brightening because of the people we'd met, especially for Anne, I was still so locked on to running as my overriding priority in life that that was all I could think about. As much as we liked it there, if things didn't start to click on the track pretty soon, it'd be too late. I had to be coached.

"Anne," I finally said one night, "I'm afraid we're going to have to go back to Kansas."

There couldn't have been a more devastating blow for her. She had just struggled back to her feet and was really beginning to enter into a number of satisfying friendships and here I was about to snatch her out of it for the sake of my running. She was willing to hang in there with me—whatever it took. We worshiped the idol of running together. Although the idol had slipped a notch in Anne's worship, it was definitely intact, in its wrongful place at the top of our priority list.

Running was the ruling god in my life. Running was everything. What was best for my track career dictated what we did. So, as we did for every move, all our possessions were stuffed into a U-Haul and off to Kansas we drove.

By this time the press had again taken up the banner of my frustration:

... and then there is Jim Ryun. Ryun, the twenty-five-year-old two-time Olympian, plagued by hay fever, defeat, and dreary miles of four minutes, or five or ten it sometimes seemed, but refusing to quit, and thereby gaining as much respect for his courage (or obstinacy) as he ever did for his world records. Ryun, bouncing pathetically from Kansas to Oregon to California and back to Kansas, ever questing for the answer. Ryun, winning one race, running a dismal next-to-last in his next, chasing victory, catching frustration. [*Sports Illustrated*, July 1972]

I had the opportunity to turn the tide of my fortunes on March 4, again in LA in the Coliseum where I'd run so many great races, in a nationally televised mile against stiff competition. At last I could vindicate myself before the nation!

But it was not to be.

The race had been run and Jim Ryun had finished forlorn and last in 4:19.2 and now, when all he wanted was to be alone, he stood in a gloomy tunnel of the Los Angeles Coliseum and answered questions. When as a Kansas schoolboy he had run the best milers of the world into the ground, the public had made him bigger than life, and even then he wondered at the insanity of it. But the public likes its heroes to be heroic and is annoyed when they are anything less, and this Jim Ryun understands. So last weekend, sick at heart, he accepted his defeat as gracefully as he had accepted his victories.

"No, I don't know what is wrong," he answered, with blank eyes. "Is it mental? Perhaps. I don't know . . . Yes, I knew when I was out of the race." A small smile appeared. "When I was 150 yards behind and everybody was pulling away from me."

"Why don't they give him a blindfold and a cigarette?" a friend said to Anne Ryun. . . . [*Sports Illustrated*, March 1972]

How I'd wanted to stop during that race! But I knew after Miami that the press would crucify me if I did it again. So I endured the humiliation, peddled slowly around the track, so far behind the rest of the field I was surprised they hadn't begun the next race. At last the final straight came. I jogged in, crossed the line, and slowed to a walk.

I thought to myself, "How can this be happening?"

I felt like I had the plague. Instead of clustering around me as they had in past years, the reporters and officials at trackside sort of backed silently away, letting me through without a word. I walked down the track a ways, stopped to untie my spikes, and walked on barefoot.

All of a sudden my anger and frustration exploded. I threw my shoes viciously down on the track and yelled, "What's wrong with me?"

I knew I was in shape. How could the performances be so erratic?

A month later the Kansas Relays provided an up moment—I ran 3:57 and spoke out confidently to the press about my troubles being behind me.

But, alas, I had spoken too soon. During the next week's race I caught a bad case of stomach cramps, about which *Sports Illustrated* added a touch of humor to the wearisome tale of Jim Ryun's woes:

There was nothing wrong with Ryun's feet, but after a week-long siege of dysentery he was not the man who ran a 3:57.1 two weeks ago in the Kansas Relays. "I'll give it my best shot," he said. He did until the second turn of the second lap and suddenly thought, "Where's the men's room?" He finished next to last in 4:09 and kept right on running to the W.C. [*Sports Illustrated*, May 1, 1972]

Two weeks later, again at the King Games in Philadelphia:

The best Jim Ryun could do in the mile run in the Martin Luther King Games was next to last. . . . The twenty-five-year-old Ryun ran 4:14.1 as Bowling Green's Dave Wottle won the event. Ryun didn't wait around to explain one of his worst performances since coming out of retirement two years ago. He doubled back about 100 yards, ran into the stands and disappeared along with his wife. [*Eugene Register-Guard*, May 15, 1972]

Of a two-mile later that season, the hometown newspaper wrote:

Some 4,000 fans watched in dumbfounded disappointment Wednesday night in Memorial Stadium as Ryun . . . turtled to a pedestrian 9:13.4 clocking in the two-mile. [*Lawrence Daily Journal-World*, August 1972]

Good grief!

Sports Illustrated wrote:

What is wrong with Jim Ryun? All us amateur Freuds in the sportswriting trade have analyzed his psyche down to the last twitch of the Id. . . . [*Sports Illustrated,* April 3, 1972]

All I had to say was "If you find out any answers, guys, let me know." I was ready to quit. Forget the Olympics forever and head for exile in Siberia!

Still I kept coming back for more races—a glutton for punishment I suppose. I actually knew no other course to take. I didn't want to give up. I wanted that gold medal!

CHAPTER 13

New Purpose in Life

Back in Kansas, the training progressed well but the frustrations continued. No matter where we turned, it seemed people kept turning up who had experienced this "new life." We had hardly been back in Kansas two weeks when another unexpected encounter thrust us still deeper into it. At last we were ready not just to listen from a distance but to begin asking if there might not be something here for us.

Anne and I love to play racketball. It had always been a part of my training program. In April of that year we played one evening with Coach Timmons and Pat along with a friend of theirs, Clara Taylor, whose husband Bernie was also on the faculty at the University of Kansas. After racketball Clara invited us over to their home for lemonade—fresh squeezed, she said. How could we refuse?

As we entered their home, Bernie greeted us warmly. There were papers scattered about the table and he'd obviously been busy at work on something.

We seated ourselves comfortably in their living room and were soon relaxed and chatting away. Pat's curiosity soon got the best of her.

"What is that you were working on, Bernie?" she asked.

"Bernie's writing an article for a national magazine," Clara said.

"Bernie!" Pat exclaimed. "I didn't know you wrote. I'd love to read it."

"I'm not quite through with it," he said, "but as soon as I am I'll let you know."

"What's it about?" asked Pat.

"How I became a Christian," said Bernie, "and my experience with the Lord."

There was a brief pause.

"Bernie," Pat continued, "I didn't know. I mean—well, when did all this happen? I guess I don't know what you mean. You've always been a Christian. You're an elder in your church, aren't you?"

"Yes, but I'd never before met Jesus in a living way until recently."

"I went to a retreat last year," Clara broke in, "and when there I discovered that going to church all my life wasn't the same as letting God's Spirit dwell inside me in a vital way. That's when I opened up and let Him in. Then I came home and told Bernie about it."

"At first," said Bernie, laughing at the memory, "it made me angry. I was dead set against all this talk of the Holy Spirit filling your heart—baptizing you with the Spirit was what Clara called it. I was hostile. It really came between us for a while."

"So did something happen to change your mind?" Pat went on, not to be deterred.

"Well, that's what the article's about."

Pat continued to probe this most unusual revelation. From what I'd seen of Bernie in the past, he was a usual athletic teacher and coach, as comfortable with locker room "jock talk" as the next guy. He was the last one I'd have expected to be discussing a religious experience. "Tell us about it," said Pat.

Timmie shifted his weight in his chair and Anne and I waited to see what would come next. There was a certain discomfort to the situation, listening to a discussion so out of the ordinary and wondering if someone would put you on the spot. Yet, though we had just met the Taylors in a personal way for the first time, there did seem to be something different about them, something distinguishing them from the crowd. Maybe we would find out what it was.

"Like I said," Bernie continued, "my first reaction was negative. But I couldn't get it out of my mind. A book had been laying around the house that Clara had brought back from the retreat. I was curious and began reading—when Clara wasn't around." He laughed. "Part of me was still mad at her. Well . . . the long and short of it is that between the book and everything Clara had said and my own growing curiosity to find out if there was anything to it, I began to pray that God would show me the answer."

"And did he?" asked Anne, growing more interested and beginning to pump him with questions along with Pat. For we had seen this life-style in Santa Barbara and wanted to know what it was.

"I went out for a drive one night," Bernie went on, "and after a while I found myself way out in the country, walking. I can't recall everything going through my mind at the time. But I do know I sensed that I had a deep need and that my spiritual life up to that point hadn't been on the solid footing I had once thought. By this point I knew that Jesus was the one who could fill that void and give purpose and direction to my life. That's when I dedicated my life to Him—something I had never done in all my active years in the church."

"What did you actually do?"

"I simply opened my heart and asked His Spirit to come into my life, to fill me, and show me how to live. That's what the Bible calls being born again in John 3:3–8."

"And that's all?" asked Pat. "It sounds too simple to have made such a big difference."

Clara passed the pitcher of lemonade around again and then said, "Becoming a Christian *is* simple and fun. Acknowledging your need for the Lord, praying that prayer inviting Him to come in and remake you . . . there's nothing to it. All it requires is a humble heart. But *living* as a Christian once you've begun . . . it's such a change."

"Change, yes," said Bernie, "but fulfilling like no other kind of life you can live. The Christian faith isn't just 'one other thing to try' that works only for *some* people. It is *the* truth. It's the only way to complete fulfillment."

All this time I hadn't said a word, but I certainly found myself participating in the discussion, even if only as a listener. Without even noticing, I'd been inching forward in my seat and was wide awake, my eyes darting back and forth following the conversation among Bernie, Clara, Pat, and Anne.

"This is fascinating!" I thought to myself. I was spellbound.

Pat continued to ply her friends with questions. "Well then, if it's so rewarding, why does it seem like a hard life to live?"

"I'm not sure hard is the right word to use. Complex maybe. I consider living the Christian life a privilege—something I *get* to do. At the same time there is a standard of life that God requires. Not a list of dos and don'ts from a church. We all grew up with that and it's nothing like what God has in mind. It gets so you want to live according to the principles of the Bible and you want to model your life after that of Jesus, following his commands and instructions and example. He loves you so much you want to return that love. You can't just accept the Lord and then live any way you choose. You must allow His Spirit, working inside you, to change your habit and behavior patterns to reflect Jesus. He came to earth to be our example, to show us how we are supposed to live."

Another pause followed.

We each sat quietly, lost in our private thoughts. I, along with Anne, had been following the course of the conversation in rapt attention. Yet I was aware that part of me was listening from a distance.

I eased back into my chair, took another sip of lemonade, and scratched my chin. Interesting, even captivating—yes. About all I was sure of at this point was that I wanted to run it all through my mind a few more times. I wasn't ready to share openly what I thought; I even found myself hesitant to ask questions. I was still wrestling with the fact that all of this wasn't really favorable and in line with my denominational upbringing. After all, I'd gone to church all my life—wasn't that good enough?

I was hungry for something that would offer our lives a deeper meaning. But "a personal relationship with Jesus" . . . that certainly represented a far cry from my childhood experience when I'd become a Christian—or so had thought.

I was twelve and had gone forward in church thinking that was what you did to "be" a Christian. Really all I'd done was become a member of the church. My only real desire at the time was to be able to pass out visitor's cards on Sunday morning like all the other boys my age got to do. It was peer pressure again—the desire to conform and be accepted.

Now here was something new, having to do with my heart and mind and emotions, not my involvement with a particular church. Clara and Bernie hadn't even *mentioned* church. It sounded so right and good, but I still wasn't sure.

Anne and I had both grown up in surroundings where church played a focal part. We'd tried to carry this over into our marriage and had tried to remain as moral and upstanding as we could. We gradually were seeing that this hadn't been enough. Did being a Christian mean not only believing things "about" Jesus but also involve allowing Him to live in our hearts to live His live through us? Did it entail obeying His principles throughout every facet of life? Such questions that had begun brewing in Santa Barbara began to come into clearer focus after the evening with Bernie and Clara.

In the weeks following I ran 3:57, 4:09, then 4:14 miles; the inner turmoil intensified daily. Poor Anne was in tears every day. When I was away for one race she called Clara, sobbing on the phone, and simply said, "Will you come over and pray with me? I'm so miserable!" This was a first—to *ask* someone to pray with you is a most humbling experience.

My insides wound tighter and tighter in knots. Every morning I awoke depressed. Timmie could hardly get two words out of me other than dour mumbling and despairing sighs. We were at the bottom. There *had* to be a change. The running ups and downs symbolized externally the disarray of my inner life.

A month or so later we made a trip out to California where I was scheduled to run a 5000-meter race in Bakersfield. Before leaving, Anne and I discussed what had been happening to us and the frustrations we were both experiencing. We'd discussed religious and spiritual topics many times in the past, but at this point we were at the end of our rope. This was no longer just a mental exercise for us. We were desperate for some solid, workable answers.

"I sometimes wonder," I said, "if we haven't been just looking for some spiritual Band-Aid to patch up my running problems."

"It seems every time I try to pray lately I'm saying, 'God, won't you please get me running consistently again?' "

"So what are you suggesting?" asked Anne.

"I don't know. After listening to Bernie and Clara, I guess I'm not sure God is handing out Band-Aids to take care of people's problems. It just seems like there's supposed to be more to it."

"I've been thinking about it too," said Anne. "I didn't want to say anything that night. But I've been kind of uncomfortable ever since. I mean, we're just like Bernie was—good people, trying to act with integrity, going to church, and all that. On the surface, it looks like we have it all together. Bernie said he wasn't a Christian at all, even after twenty years in church."

Our eyes met momentarily, but neither of us spoke. We both sensed, I think, that Anne had hit the nail right on the head. In the true sense of the word, we *weren't* Christians. For a solution to come, no one-time Band-Aid would do. The Lord wanted us—*all* of us. Our inner unrest was His way of trying to get our attention. We had never allowed His Spirit, as Bernie had found, to actually come to reside in our hearts to baptize us. We realized that was the distinctive difference between us and Neil, Brother Andrew, Jay and

Susan, the Hermans, Anne's sister Cate, all the Christians we'd been drawn to in Santa Barbara, and now Bernie and Clara.

We had been stubborn, and so prideful. Finally, at long last, our ears began to unplug and His voice started to come through.

We sat awhile longer in silence. Finally I blurted out to Anne, almost in desperation: "We know our life's been a mess. We know we both want this new life we've been hearing about. We both want to be Christians. And we want to *live* as Christians. We do want God's Spirit in our hearts. Okay, let's do something about it."

That night we called our friends, Susan and Jay, in Santa Barbara. "I have a race in Bakersfield," I said. "We'd . . . we'd really like to talk. Do you suppose we could stay with you, and maybe have Father Bob from the church over?"

"Sure," they said.

"There are some things on our minds and, well . . . we really need you to pray for us."

They willingly agreed to set it up for the night prior to the race.

When we arrived in Santa Barbara, we had dinner with Jay and Susan and the pastor of their church, Father Bob. After dinner we got up from the table and made our way into the living room. I have to admit that I was somewhat apprehensive. I knew full well that I, in a sense, had called the meeting and that there was no backing out now.

I slumped down in a great overstuffed chair. Everyone else sat down, and there was a moment's silence. I took a deep breath, and said: "Ever since we met you people and others like you, Anne and I knew there was something different at work in your lives. But it's only been recently, just in the last couple of months, that we finally faced up to the fact that . . . well, that we don't possess the life inside that you do. We have been miserable these past few years. We have been searching without even knowing it. We finally have reached the point of knowing that we want the life you have. So would you pray over us and ask God's Spirit to come into our hearts and fill us?"

"We would be blessed . . . honored to do so," said Father Bob immediately.

Jay and Susan rose from their seats and walked to where I sat. Anne was sitting on the floor beside me. Each of the three laid their hands on me and began to pray. "Lord, we thank you for Jim and give you praise for his openness to you. And now we ask that your

Spirit would enter his heart and dwell there and fill him with your goodness and love."

As they prayed, I prayed along silently.

The moment they laid their hands on Anne and began praying for her in a similar fashion, she began weeping freely. Someone handed her a box of Kleenex that she put on the floor beside her. She continued to cry and cry and within an hour the box was empty. The floodgate to her heart had been supernaturally opened, releasing the years of hurt, pain, resentment, and real emptiness.

They continued to pray very softly and encouraged us to join in, thanking God for His love and what He had done. I had never prayed aloud in a group like this but soon found myself beginning to speak. Suddenly an enormous peace swept over me and I found deep expressions of prayer pouring forth out of my inner being.

Later that night, as we lay in bed, I could sense that something dramatic had taken place. I remembered Jay's words as we had been praying together: "Don't worry so much about whether you *feel* anything. You may, you may not. The important thing to remember is that when you pray for the Lord's Spirit to come into your heart, He does. You'll never be the same again. For He'll immediately go to work to begin transforming you from the inside out."

So while I didn't feel a great tingle of excitement, yet there remained a peace deep inside. Something told me my athletic career had, in one sense, ended that night. It had died. It was no longer to be my idol, my god. Jesus would fill that emptiness. For so many years there had been a relentless striving—and toward what? The whole basis for running changed that night. I knew something had happened to me.

However, in my typically cautious manner, the reserved part of me still wanted to wait and see what would happen. I had felt times of peace before. So as I lay there in bed I thought to myself, "The key will be if the peace is still there tomorrow, and the next day. That will be the test of whether this is real. Then I'll know this isn't just a passing fancy, heightened by the emotional events of the evening."

With those thoughts, I drifted off to sleep.

When I awoke the following morning, I was surprised to find that the peace of the night before was still with me. As we drove over to Bakersfield, I was quiet and thoughtful the whole way, still extremely content and relaxed inside, wondering what the implications were of what we had done. What, I wondered further, would inviting the Lord into my heart mean in my running? The year had been such a disaster thus far. Would this new peace of mind settle my emotions to the point where I'd begin running with consistency again?

The field for the 5000-meter run was strong and with my inexperience in the event I was uncertain about my chances of doing well. I wound up third in 13:38.2—a second and a half behind the leaders. I was elated. It had been easy and was a tremendous confidence-builder, by far my best 5000 time ever.

In my heart I was thankful. I felt God had given me a small sign that He was watching and caring for me, a confirmation that we were now heading the right way. So much stress had been brought to bear on my life. At last I was beginning to see that it had all been used to prepare me for God's intervention in a more direct way.

It was not by any means that all of life's rough spots vanished. There continued to be frustrations. It took Anne several months to surrender her life to the Lord completely. Yet we slowly came to view life from a new perspective. We began asking about God's purpose in things. We didn't know exactly what Christians were "supposed" to do. No one took us aside, sat us down, and said, "This is how you grow in the life of faith." So we tested the waters, prayed together occasionally, read the Bible sporadically (not knowing how to go about it,) and went once in a while to Christian bookstores to find more books about this Christian life we wanted to be part of. All the while, as the Munich Olympics approached still nearer, the peace that had flooded me that night remained.

CHAPTER 14

The Eugene Trials

My new-found peace in being a Christian did indeed carry over onto the track! Because I was content within myself, suddenly the pieces began to fit back together. The Olympic Trials for Munich were now a month away, to be held in Eugene of all places—the center of my earlier allergy problems. The way things had been going so far this year, in a month . . . who could tell? I might be running miles of 3:48 . . . or 4:37!

Somehow though, I was confident the bad races were behind me. Anne was now pregnant (with our twin sons, Drew and Ned), and as the Olympics drew ever closer, it began to dawn on us that here was a real opportunity to live more visibly the life we wanted to. We had accepted God's love, but we really didn't know what to do with it yet. There was already such a difference in our outlook on life that we wanted to share it even though we knew so little. Therefore, we saw the Games as a way to glorify God in our lives. What better way to share the peace I'd found than by being the gold medalist and saying, "God helped get me here"!

The new-found spiritual direction did not come all at once, in a bright flash of inspiration. We did not become fanatical street-preaching evangelists. The process was slow. We simply began taking God's ways seriously. We read the Bible like a manual, a handbook on how to live according to God's ways and promises. Our belief and faith began to grow slowly.

Despite all the ups and downs, I felt strong physically and thus planned to enter two events at the Eugene Olympic Trials. I hadn't raced enough in recent years, however, during which time the 800-meter competition had become fast and fierce, and I was not alert in my racing techniques. In a race that short, one mistake and you're dead.

I made it through the early rounds of qualification all right, but in the final I made the supreme tactical blunder. The pace was quick and I knew everyone else had strong kicks. Therefore on the back straightaway, with about 300 yards to go, I made a mad dash around the field and broke into a full sprint. I flew down the backstretch, covering 200 meters in 24 seconds, and opened up a huge lead on the rest of the field.

Coming out of the final turn, I realized I had moved 50 or 60 yards too soon. My legs gradually turned to putty, then to lead, and behind me the field was gaining rapidly! I had been beaten at my own game and had pushed Dave Wottle to a world-record-tying run of 1:44.3. Dave and two others caught me just short of the finish, and I missed making the team by a nose in 1:45.2.

That evening I called Anne at her parent's home in Ohio where she was visiting before flying out for the 1500 meters. She was furious.

"How dare you lose after we've worked so hard for this?"

I tried to apologize and calm her down, but it was no use. Besides, I felt bad enough myself.

Finally Timmie interrupted the conversation.

"Hand me the phone," he said.

I did so gladly.

"Anne, honey," he said in his most soothing, fatherly tone, "listen. Jim ran a fast race, and a good time."

"But he lost!"

"I know. But he hasn't run many 800's lately. He's just a bit out of practice, that's all. Besides, this was just a tune-up for the 1500. He'll do fine. You just settle down, don't worry about a thing, and we'll be looking forward to seeing you out here."

He shot a quick wink at me, signaling that he had settled the ruffled feathers back into place.

Wottle had run brilliantly and would probably have beaten me anyway. I'd run a stupid race and couldn't help feeling low.

I knew I'd reached the end of the line. For five years I'd been struggling to regain the top of the mountain. My career during that time read like a comedy of errors. Now here I was with one final shot at making good. This was my last hurrah. There was no tomorrow.

In the 1500 I determined that *nothing* was going to go wrong. No more blunders. No more paces I couldn't handle. No more foolish premature sprints. "I'm going to control these races," I thought.

"These guys will all be watching me, so I'm going to keep them guessing, off their toes."

I decided that to whatever extent I could, I was going to control the tempo of the heats. I wanted no surprises! I wasn't about to take any chances.

So as we lined up at the starting line for the first round of qualification, I was ready to do something I rarely did. The moment the gun fired, I jumped quickly into the lead. But I instantly backed off and set a nice, slow pace. Everyone else followed, no one wanted to challenge me, and so there I stayed. I picked an easy pace I was comfortable with and that's where we all ran. The strategy seemed to catch everyone off guard. I could imagine the sportscasters exclaiming, "Ladies and gentlemen, I really don't know what to say. This truly has to be one of the most unexpected turns of events in the Trials thus far. Jim Ryun, if you can believe it . . . is *leading* the race!"

Around the track we ran, everyone else just settling in behind me. From such a commanding position, especially being able to dictate the pace, I was able to tell what was going on all throughout the race. Toward the end I picked it up, sprinted down the straightaway, and had no problem finishing in front.

The next day I determined to run the semifinal heat in precisely the same manner. I did so and it developed along exactly the same lines. I led from the start to finish.

Then came the finals. By this time, Anne had joined me in Eugene. Trying to pray more regularly together now, we both asked God to allow me to make the team.

Only the top three would make the Olympic team, and I was more resolute than ever. I didn't want this last chance to be a swan song. I would have run through a brick wall on that day I was so determined to do what I had to do.

I went out onto the infield, did my final warm-up, and then got ready to take off my sweats. I grabbed and pulled them down nearly to my knees before I realized my hands had latched onto *everything*, trunks and all, revealing my bent-over posterior in all its white, glistening, splendor. I quickly pulled my trunks back up, but not before the crowd had had both an eyeful and a good chuckle. The ice was broken and it added some levity to the drama of the upcoming race.

Walking toward the starting line, I knew basically how I wanted to approach the race. I also knew I had made some tactical blunders in the past that had proved very costly. I silently prayed, "Jesus, I give you this race. If things don't go according to plan, give me wisdom to react quickly and carefully. I leave the results in your hands." That was the beginning of my learning to trust God for His best for me.

My plan was simple, but it was exactly the opposite strategy from what I had done in the heats. This time I wasn't about to take the lead. It was back to the same scenario that had always worked in prior years—follow until the last 200 or 300 yards—and then go for it!

By now, as a result of the qualifying rounds, the other competitors were watching for me to jump into the front and establish the pace. Therefore no one else was prepared to take charge after the gun sounded. So once again I caught them off guard and the pace was very slow (62, 2:05.4). I just sat comfortably back toward the end of the pack. I was determined to sit on it until I *knew* that it was the right time and that I could hold a stretch drive all the way. Wottle was in the field again, and I had by now grown very respectful of his finishing speed.

Around and around we went, tightly clustered, everyone aware that it was going to come down to a final sprint and hoping against hope that on this particular day *my* kick would prove good enough. Still the pace lagged.

The gun lap came and the pace quickened, but still no one broke. Three hundred yards to go and still nine runners were bunched in a space of five yards; 250 yards to go and still no one made a move.

"What is this?" I said to myself. "Are we all just going to lope on in like this? I *know* I can hold on for 250 yards!"

So I bolted around the field. I knew behind me the race was on!

Around the curve and into the straight we all flew, covering the final quarter in 51 seconds. I glanced hurriedly back but had opened up ten yards. Looking back down the track, I was closing in on the finish line and joy welled up inside me.

Sportswriters cough, sputter, and blanch these days when someone begins cliché-ing about the pressures of Olympic athletes . . . but the pressure was real . . . at the Olympic track-and-field trials in Eugene . . . and it bore down on no one more heavily than the recently uncertain Jim Ryun.

It is an amazing tribute to the stature of Ryun that he has remained such a universally popular figure through a period as full of trauma, problems and yes—outright failures as have shadowed him through the uncertain months of his comeback attempt.

And the undercurrent of "inside" stories has made its rounds from coast to coast among fellow athletes, sportswriters, television producers, AAU officials and fans. Few were complimentary and most reflected badly on those surrounding Jim these days. But curiously, most of them explained those things that troubled Ryun to the point that he no longer could succeed. They rationalized his losses.

Even his critics handled Jim Ryun with respect.

And the jam-packed crowds in Eugene's Hayward Field were as partisan in his quest for a place on the U.S. Olympic team as they were for their own hometown, favorite Oregonians . . .

So Ryun brought with him unusual backing in what for many personal reasons was the biggest race of his life. For not only were there the pressures of the Olympic Trials—perhaps bigger for many than the games themselves.

But there were the pressures of the months of uncertainties, of poor races, of unexplainable triumphs and failures, of circumstances that even Jim and his coach, Bob Timmons, did not fully understand.

And there was the failure in the 800-meter race the week before.

Jim Ryun brought all those to the starting line with him at Eugene in a test that almost everyone in the stands understood was a test of far more than speed over 1500 meters.

Track and field, perhaps because of its personal individualism, is the most emotional sport of all and it is not unusual to see even blase officials wiping their eyes following a thrilling race or achievement.

The magnetism of Ryun, diminished not at all in recent months, combined with the spectre of America's biggest track meet in four years, had brought the crowd to a near-frenzy and from the moment the contestants were introduced, the din was growing toward its emotional climax.

When Jim Ryun sprinted into the lead coming out of the final turn, the roar was continuous and ear-shattering. Officials were waving their stopwatches. The sportswriters of six nations were all standing at their desks —sometimes on top of them.

And as Ryun neared the finish line, he threw his hands high and burst into the widest grin of his twenty-five years. Across the line . . . with fists raised high, he motioned to the crowd which cheered wildly for minutes after the race. Never before has Jim Ryun showed his feelings so openly.

It was one of those rare moments in sport—in life—in which 19,000 persons shared vicariously in triumph. [Rich Clarkson, *Topeka Capital-Journal*, July 17, 1972]

After my 1500-meter win at the 1972 Olympic Trials
I was exultant as trainer Barry Ryan assisted me off
the track.

1. Jim Ryun	3:41.5
2. Dave Wottle	3:42.3
3. Bob Wheeler	3:42.4
4. Jerome Howe	3:43.0
5. Howell Michael	3:43.0
6. Duncan MacDonald	3:43.8
7. Reggie McAfee	3:44.1

I was ecstatic . . . never before had there been so satisfying a race.
I was higher than a kite in April . . . I mean, I was happy! I knew

God had blessed me that day, for that race. Inside my heart I said, "Thank you, Lord!"

ABC was broadcasting live and immediately after the race began making efforts to get me in front of their camera, which under *these* circumstances I couldn't have been happier about. It was one of those moments of great elation when I wanted to give the credit to the Lord, Timmie, Anne, and everyone who stuck by me through the ups and downs.

It wound up being ten minutes before the interview could actually begin. Though there remained a constant hubbub about me and though I was far too exultant to stop moving, laughing, shaking hands, smiling, and waving at the crowd still cheering, within that time frame—as if life momentarily stood still—a torrent of thoughts rushed through my brain. All around me the world suddenly stilled, while I was able to look about and reflect on everything that had happened.

A rush of thanksgiving poured out of my spirit.

There was Timmie . . . standing beside me like a proud father. How fortunate I'd been to have him as a coach. Such a good man. So soft-spoken, yet tough and determined. So steady and loyal. He'd been the prime driving force in my life for so long. Fate could easily have sent me a far different kind of man. Timmie made me believe in myself, pushed me to heights none of us would have dreamed possible, and—perhaps most importantly of all—solidified within me a picture of integrity itself. He'd lost a few hairs during 1968 and a few more this spring. What a year it had been—beating Keino indoors, then a 4:19, a 3:57, a 4:14, another 3:57 mile. Yet when others had given up on me, Timmie kept gently encouraging, never stopped believing, and helped me to believe in myself once again.

What affection I felt for Him, now in this moment of celebration that few others could share in as completely as He.

And Anne . . . "Lord, where would I be without Anne?" So many wives make it difficult for their husbands. After all, why should wives care about sports and athletic careers? But there she was, never giving up on me, never losing her confidence in the person she saw inside me, willing to verbally dress me down when I needed it, encourage me when I needed that, always supportive of what I wanted to do, realizing how much it all meant to me and to us. How she'd lived out her love for me, and how deeply I loved her!

A year . . . four years . . . had culminated in this one moment of victory as it all flashed through my mind. The road back had been so rocky and arduous. Somehow I had hung on, and had made it—with Anne's help, with Timmie's help, and with the Lord's help.

The sounds of commotion gradually filtered back into my brain. I was still smiling and waving, the crowd still cheering. It was all I could do to keep the tears of joy from flooding my eyes.

I was at last only one rung away from the end of the quest.

CHAPTER 15

Battling the Bureaucracy

Anne and I were excited about Munich. Things had been clicking as they hadn't for years. Training progressed well. No mono, no altitude, no severe allergy problems. The times around the world weren't that remarkable and in the major forecasts I was increasingly coming to be regarded as the favorite. Anne and I were more and more convinced that the Lord was responsible for the turnaround and found ourselves eager to say so publicly.

I had raced well so infrequently throughout the season that Timmie felt we needed some measuring stick to see where I was. Therefore we went to Toronto at the end of July for a mile in the Metro Toronto Police Games. After an evenly paced race, I took over with about a lap and a half to go and finished in a relatively easy 3:52.8. Ironically, though this time would come back to haunt me at the Games, it was the third fastest mile ever run, behind my two world records.

At last I knew I'd returned to peak form . . . I was ready! The press once again began building American hopes for the first 1500 gold medal in decades.

Interviewed after the Toronto race, I said, "I like to think it is a faith in God that has helped me. I've found a personal relationship with Jesus Christ, something that has been lacking before." My words were quoted in coverage of the race, and I anticipated that the gold medal would give further opportunities to tell the world about our new-found relationship with the Lord. After all, we reasoned, if we had spent all these years searching for Jesus, wouldn't it help others find Him more easily with less heartache if we told them of our discovery?

For the first time in years I felt confident. The pilgrimage was at last nearly over. I knew when the Olympic final came, Kip would go out strong and force the race. It would be an exact duplicate of Mexico, but this time I could stick with him. With his early pace and the kick I was once again sure of, there was hardly a question in my mind we'd force the race close to 3:30—the approximate equivalent of a 3:46 mile. One of us was ready to do it. It would indeed bring the rivalry to a thrilling conclusion!

A premonition of things to come arrived a few days before Olympic competition was to begin. When the U.S. distance coach Ted Haydon presented me with my heat assignment, I took one look at it and was dismayed.

"But Ted," I said, "they've put me in Keino's heat. That's against the seeding rules."

"I know. The computer fouled up and interpreted your Toronto 3:52 mile as a 1500-meter time."

"But they can't have the two top-ranked runners in the same heat," I protested.

"The computer doesn't know that. It thinks you're the slowest in the field."

"Can't we contest it?"

"Don't worry," insisted Ted. "It's not that big a deal. No sense creating waves if we don't have to. You know how these officials are."

"But it could be significant," I answered.

"Relax," he replied. "You'll do fine. You'll qualify with a 3:45."

"I see your point," I said finally. Maybe Ted was right. I had but to place fourth. Even with Keino in the race, how difficult could that be?

Circumstances then began to unfold that rendered singleness of focus on my race gradually more difficult.

For quite some time I'd been taking medication for my allergies. Dr. Keystone, who had accompanied me to Munich, had months earlier written to the IOC's official medical advisor and had obtained the list of authorized medications. He'd planned my treatment accordingly.

Three days prior to my first heat, we learned that swimming gold medalist Rick DeMont was being stripped of his medal because illegal medication had been discovered in his body. He was being treated for asthma with drugs similar to those I had been taking for my allergies.

Jay suggested we discontinue my medication immediately.

"But I thought it was all covered, with that list we received from the IOC doctor." I said.

"So did I," answered Jay. "But I'm not so sure about these lists anymore. I don't want to trust our fate to them, because . . . who knows, they might have issued a *new* list of allowed medications by now, one we've never seen. No, I really think we ought to get you off everything."

Dr. Keystone was referring to a foul-up that had caused Eddie Hart (the favorite) and Rey Robinson to miss their heats of the 100 meters and to lose a chance for the medals they probably would have won. Their coach had a schedule for the races, sent the sprinters to the stadium on time, only to discover that the heats were already over. The schedules had been changed, then changed again, then again. Their coach, Stan Wright, had not been notified and publicly said, "The organization in Munich was the most pathetic I've ever seen."

Nothing would be done to rectify the error. Though there were lane openings in another heat that would easily have allowed Robinson and Hart a chance to compete, the United States was not one of the more popular contingencies, and Wright's pleas went ignored.

"What about my allergies?" I asked Dr. Keystone finally.

"We'll just have to hope you'll be okay," he replied.

Bob Seagren, still the pole-vault world-record holder, was the next to be stung at the hands of officialdom. Because there was some question about whether he would be allowed to use a new "banana" pole or an older model fiberglass pole, he came prepared with both types—three new poles, six old. The newer poles in general were somewhat lighter, fully regulation, and had been made available to all the world's vaulters several months earlier. However, when the Games opened there were complaints against the lighter poles on the part of the East German vaulters, led by their leading star Wolfgang Nordwig, who maintained that the Americans using them would be capitalizing on an advantage. Therefore, throughout the qualification rounds Bob had to keep switching poles while the International Amateur Athletic Federation (IAAF) officials banned, unbanned, and rebanned the various types of poles being used.

Trying to add a touch of levity to Bob's dilemma, George Young,

Ted Haydon, and I found a huge poster of three orangutan apes, bought it, and took it to Bob's room. One of the chimps was holding a long pole, like a fence post. On the bottom we inscribed "Want to use my pole, Bob?" It helped ease the tension, if only for a moment!

Just before the final, the IAAF officials entered his room while he was absent and confiscated all nine of his poles and ultimately Nordwig got the gold medal. Such an uproar was raised that the Olympic issue of *Track & Field News* devoted seven full pages to a detailed recounting of the entire fiasco. People were angry!

An equally controversial decision by the IOC involved 400-meter gold and silver medalists Vince Matthews and Wayne Collett. On the victory stand, reminiscent of Tommie Smith and John Carlos in 1968 with their black-gloved fists in the air, they casually chatted, slouched, and fidgeted during the national anthem rather than standing solemnly at attention. Though they'd broken no specific rule and claimed to have no particular protest in mind, the IOC termed their behavior "disgusting" and summarily banished the two from any future Olympic competition. Notwithstanding that the behavior in question was in poor taste, there was neither precedent nor rule justifying the Committee's action. Thus U.S. chances for an almost certain win in the 1600-meter relay were arbitrarily eliminated.

By this time great anger had been kindled among our American athletes, directed not only against the IOC, but also against the U.S. coaching staff and the U.S. Olympic Committee for their contribution to the problems. After a week in Germany I headed down to Mittenwald to visit Anne where she was lodging with her parents for a day or two. We went to dinner at the Green Door Restaurant on the military base there. Midway through our meal, a waiter approached me.

"Mr. Ryun?" he said.

I nodded.

"Have you heard of the events at the Olympic Village?"

"No," I answered.

With that, he proceeded to sketch the terrifying takeover by terrorists of the Israeli section of the living quarters and the death of eleven athletes.

I was stunned. As soon as possible, I called back to Munich and managed to reach my roommate George Young.

"George," I asked, "what's the situation there? I was planning to come back tonight."

"Don't!" said George. "It's tense. German soldiers armed with machine guns on every street corner. Everyone's jumpy, wondering what's going to happen next. I'd stay there until things cool down a little."

I hung up the phone and walked slowly back to tell Anne I'd be staying with them another night. As it turned out, the Games were to be delayed a day for a memorial service for the Israelis and then resumed the next day. Anne and I questioned at the time whether or not the Olympics should even be resumed at all. In fact, we spent much time in prayer and discussion as to what my posture should be. The Israeli situation (of particular interest to us as Christians who love God's chosen people, coupled with Anne's dream of my falling during my semifinal heat,) stirred up much questioning in our hearts. In fact, given more time and maturity, I may not have run at all. But being caught up in the moment, we followed through with our original strategy.

As my first preliminary heat neared, my mind was cluttered with conflicting feelings about the week thus far. My workouts went well. In one session I ran two 1:51 800s with only three minutes between them. I felt *very* good and only hoped everything would go more smoothly for me than it had thus far for my teammates.

After the first week, *Time* magazine made the following comments on the progress of the Games:

The second week of the XX Olympiad proceeded under a grim penumbra cast not only by the brutal murders, but by sloppy officiating, errant decisions by Brundage's International Olympic Committee, and by the insensitivity of Brundage himself. . . . The multinational gerontocracy of the wealthy sportsmen who run the IOC has never been particularly noted for collective brilliance. As the competitors tried to pick up the shards of the Olympiad, the committee members seemed to outdo themselves in demonstrating their skill at letter-of-the-law Pecksniffery. Unfortunately for the U.S. team, the brunt of their questionable decisions was born by American athletes who were deprived of . . . possibly three gold medals. [*Time*, September 18, 1972]

After breakfast the morning of my first heat I rested in my room until it was time. Ted Haydon accompanied Dave Wottle, Bob

Wheeler, and me to the warm-up track to begin preparation for our three individual races. I jogged around slowly, stretched, then jogged some more.

Anne's words of the night before still rang in my ears: "God be with you, Jim."

How could those five short words capture the moment? I'd been pointing toward this day for years. Suddenly it was here—the culmination of everything my life had stood for, the springboard into everything I hoped the future would hold. There was but one last pinnacle to be reached. All I had to do was win!

I stretched first my right thigh, then my left. A little tightness in the left calf . . . but it will be fine.

I tried to block out of my mind the headlines of this morning's sports page—"Ryun Favored in First 1500 Heat." Lost in my own thoughts, I spoke not a word to the others, dropped my bag of gear, glanced at my watch, sighed deeply, then eased myself down on the grass and closed my eyes.

Munich!

"Here I am!" I thought. The moment had arrived.

It had been six years since my first 3:51 mile world record. There had been the defeat by Keino in Mexico, my semiretirement, then the struggle to come back with unbelievably sporadic times. I'd run mile times covering a broad spectrum of 27 seconds, hardly encouraging for a supposed world-class athlete. Just making this 1972 Olympic team had been a remarkable victory.

But all that was now past.

I was ready and in shape. I was ready not only to win head-to-head against Keino but primed to go after the Olympic and world records as well. The achievements I had so dreamed of lay so close within my grasp. In just a few more days . . .

I stood up, pulled my U.S.A. singlet over my head, and pinned my number onto the front. "Why did they give me such an enormous singlet?" I asked myself. "This was designed for a shot-putter or hammer-thrower!" Nevertheless, I continued my preparation, lacing up my racing spikes and beginning to jog again. As before every competition, my stomach was a jumble of nerves. The race was approaching and right now—for this moment in time—nothing else mattered.

At last I heard the call for my race over the loudspeaker. I made my way through the tunnel into the main Olympic stadium where my warm-up suit was taken by the officials. Then they led us to the starting line.

As I walked to the line, the officials held up the starter just at the last minute. Someone was complaining in German and pointing to my number. Apparently they couldn't read it, I was told. The jersey was so big that as I'd pinned it on and then tucked in my shirt, part of the number was now stuck down inside my trunks. I'd have to take it off and repin it higher up. So while everyone waited, I did just that.

Another small annoyance. Hopefully . . . *now* at last everything was taken care of. I lined up, awaiting the gun, if not as composed as I would have liked to be, nonetheless still feeling good.

With the crack of the pistol, the unknown Pakistani Mohamed Younis jumped into the lead. He was clearly an entrant whose only hope of survival lay in a miraculous effort, and he gave it everything he had. As we circled the track for the first lap, he made a gallant effort. He was a courageous runner and was determined not to give up easily. The rest of the pack, including Keino and myself, followed a few yards back in a comfortable rhythm.

Nothing could have pleased me more than the slow pace; I wanted to run no faster than necessary. We circled the track again and still Younis, tiring, clung to the lead at 800 meters. Down the backstretch Keino moved around me, past the rest of the pack, and quickly into the lead. I knew if I went with him, everyone else in the field—seeing Keino in front and me bearing down on him—would get nervous and a horse race would result. So I continued to wait.

The rabbit's pace began to falter and the trailing group of us, following Keino's lead, inched closer and one by one began to move around him. Midway through the bottom curve with about 500 yards to go in the race, from my position midway through the passing crowd, I eased alongside the wavering pacesetter with Billy Fordjour from Ghana just to my right moving with me. I felt good, the tempo was relaxed. My mind was occupied with nothing more than holding the pace and moving out gradually as the final straightaway came closer.

By the time five or six runners had passed him, apparently Younis decided he'd taken enough. He wasn't about to buckle under no matter how tired he felt. Breezing along just to his right I hardly noticed him as I came up on his right shoulder. I'd passed fading runners in similar circumstances dozens of times, never thinking a thing of it. But this day was to be different.

Unexpectedly disaster struck. Without warning, suddenly I was lying on the ground. I had no idea what had happened.

When I groggily began to come to my senses, several things forced themselves into my blurred consciousness. I was bleeding and became dimly aware of another fallen runner, Fordjour of Ghana, struggling on the track beside me. Though it would be some time before I'd stop to identify the bruises on my legs and the blood on my knees and spiked foot, then I was cognizant only of intense pain throughout my body—hands, legs, arms, head—pain more severe than I'd ever remembered. Lastly, though all these sensations shot through my muddled mind in a mere fraction of a second, looking up I could see men moving along the track a quarter of a lap ahead.

"My God," I thought, "the race! Lord, the race! Help me—"

Instinct forced me to my feet. Unconsciously Timmie's words rang through the distorted images of my brain, words from the distant past: "If ever you fall, jump up. Make up the ground quickly. Get back into the competition!"

My legs throbbed in pain. My ankle was sprained, though I hardly knew it. There was no time to think. I hobbled a few steps, tried to accelerate as best I could, and tore off down the track. Energy mounted and I ran with the wind.

Seldom aware of the crowd during a race, I suddenly felt the awesome, somber hush that had descended on the more than 80,000 spectators. They'd seen and watched in stunned silence as I'd fallen, crashed my head against the metal guardrail, and lay senseless on the track, fully unconscious for perhaps eight or ten seconds.

Anne sat in the stands in a benumbed trance. Her family began to scream, along with thousands, "Get up! Get up!"

Time was ticking off—ten seconds . . . twelve . . . I managed to regain my feet. . . . thirteen . . . fifteen . . .

As I took off down the track the stands had hushed, anticipating what would come next. The race against fate appeared hopeless.

They knew I could not humanly hope to catch the other runners. So they sat noiselessly, watching the drama of my vain effort unfold.

Gradually I felt their silence changing to clapping, then cheering. Louder it grew. Somehow, through the agony and the utter impossi-

Unexpectedly disaster struck . . .

Around the track after the other runners I sprinted, still in a daze, hardly conscious of the fact I would soon know all too well—that the long quest had ended in an agonizing tumble to the ground.

At the finish I could hardly stand on my injured foot and leg.

After the race Kip tried to console me with a kindly arm around my shoulder, while photographers scurried to immortalize the poignant scene.

bility of my desperation sprint, I knew they were cheering for me! Encouraging me to do what no runner could have done.

All that final lap they cheered and I ran. I flew to the sounds of their support . . .

But it was futile. A gallant effort, but I could catch no one.

I crossed the line, still too much in a daze to recall the poignant picture I would later see in papers and magazines of Kip Keino, even as a tear was falling from my eye, with his hand on my shoulder offering what silent consolation was possible.

Before I had time to come to my senses, I was ushered off the track and back through the tunnel. Anne was there waiting. How she'd walked unhindered through the maze of officials neither of us ever knew. As I saw her, neither of us said a word, only embraced.

Somewhere from beyond the realm of human suffering and tears there came the words, "Lord . . . help us!"

CHAPTER 16

The Appeal

Out of the stadium I passively followed those around me and was soon in the hands of the team doctor who began to nurse my wounds. "Pack that leg and foot in ice tonight, Jim," he said. "You're going to be mighty sore tomorrow."

All around were coaches, officials, and friends asking, "What happened? Were you kicked . . . shoved . . . cut in front of?" The word *foul* was floating around the edges of the many simultaneous conversations.

My only reply was "I don't know. I was running along smoothly one minute and the next was flat on the track. It happened so instantly, I really don't know what exactly went on."

"It has to be a foul," I heard someone say. "There's a spike hole in his shoe, splattered with blood."

"Someone had to cut in front of him for that to happen," said another.

"It's a foul, all right. Anything that hinders another's stride is a foul—that's what the rule book says!"

There were already people getting up a petition to the Olympic Committee stating that I'd been tripped. But reports conflicted. In ABC's live telecast, all anyone could tell for certain was that I'd fallen. Nobody knew why. Head Olympic coach Bill Bowerman assured me I'd be reinstated.

That evening, back in my Olympic Village dorm room, Anne packed my leg in ice. I was dismayed. "How could I let this happen?" I thought. Even though I hoped they'd let me into the semifinals, I was concerned that I'd be too sore and stiff to run anywhere near optimum level.

But even then, though we were hardly aware of it, God was

moving in to help us in answer to our prayer as we left the stadium. Anne's family was there with us, supportive but not interfering, loving us, experiencing the hurt; and my family shared the devastation as well.

Later in the evening the door opened and in walked Ted Haydon. His face was blank.

"They denied the petition," he said. "They said they didn't feel there was sufficient evidence to indicate a foul had taken place."

"But my foot was bleeding," I argued.

"I know, Jim," said Ted, "but what can we do?"

I sighed and said nothing. After further attempts to console me, Ted left the room. Anne and I looked at each other.

"It's not fair," said Anne. "Doesn't he know what we've been through to get here?"

"I didn't trip over my own feet," I muttered half to myself.

"Maybe I should write out a petition of my own," I finally said. Howard Cosell's name kept coming into my mind. We'd always hit it off fairly well. As a lawyer, I thought he might be able to help somehow. I called him at his downtown Munich hotel where I knew the ABC staff was staying. Before long I was discussing with Howard the best way to go about drafting a petition.

The committee barely read my paper. They'd already had far too much flack from this whining American team with their complaints of injustices and their requests for special allowances.

"I can't believe it," I said to Anne. "These guys are supposed to love athletics, the ideal of fair competition."

"But can't you see what it looks like to them—the prima donna Americans, always getting their way. It's just too bad you're not from some poor, struggling, underdeveloped nation. You're *the* big name. You've been on top. They're not going to give guys like you and Seagren any breaks. If anything, they're going to be tougher on you."

She was right. We had heard that the African Mike Boit had been declared guilty of a foul in an 800-meter heat and barred from continuing. We had also heard that the committee had been petitioned on his behalf; and he'd been reinstated and allowed to move on in the competition.

With bitterness I recalled the frustrating conversation I'd had with an Olympic official. "No evidence of a foul," he had said.

"Look at my shoe," I had insisted, gesturing toward it with my hand. "It has a spike hole in it. Look at my bandaged foot. I have a gash there from another man's spikes. There's no possible way to spike yourself on the outside of your foot. According to the rules, if another touches you or interrupts your stride, it's a foul."

Refusing to glance downward at my foot, I sensed he was trying not to listen. His tone seemed to reveal a contempt for me. Then he made a statement I would long remember:

"Look, I fell in a race in the Olympics once. No one gave me another chance. I simply had to come back four years later, which I did. And may I suggest, Mr. Ryun," he added in a voice which felt distinctly colder, "that you do the same."

Anne and I looked at him incredulously, then at each other.

"Another four years!" we both exclaimed, in disbelief.

"Be reasonable," the official went on. "Even if there was a foul —I thought I'd been fouled once too—we still couldn't do anything. It would stir up too much controversy. I know the rules allow for a reinstatement, but it's too unprecedented, too open for contention by other nations. Foul or no foul, we've never done such a thing before, and we're not about to start now."

He turned away, leaving Anne and me staring after him with disbelief. Anne and I held each other and I wept openly.

Four more years . . .

We'd already spent what seemed a lifetime just getting this far. I couldn't keep running forever. We had responsibilities to think of. Four more years—it was inconceivable.

The doctor was right. The day after the fall I could hardly move.

To say I was not heartbroken when the semifinal race came and went would not be true. I was miserably depressed!

The final of the 1500-meter run was to have been one of the few events broadcast live by ABC back to the United States. It had been built up to such epic proportions, heralded as the climax of the Games with all the drama of the rematch of the decade. It had all the right ingredients and such had been ABC's design . . .

. . . until I fell.

Suddenly the fall itself became a major news story in a very plagued Olympic Games. In an effort to retain the intensity of interest they knew was present, ABC frantically regrouped their efforts. They'd caught wind of the talk of a foul and possible reinstatement, the petitions and meetings, and these factors ABC continued to discuss on the air despite all official denials.

The night before the final, I received a phone call in my room. It was Dick Ebersole from ABC.

"Jim," he said, "there may be developments."

"I'm listening," I said.

"We've just obtained a video of your heat—from the German DOZ network. I think you should see it. Can you come right over?"

"Sure," I said, perking up. "Anne's here. We'll get Timmie and get over there as soon as we can."

I sensed drama in Dick's tone. He hadn't committed himself but I could tell something important was at stake.

Before long, Anne, Timmie, and I were seated in the ABC booth with Dick. The video they'd been given had been taken from an angle that none of us had seen previously. We watched the race develop and the crucial moment drew near.

"Okay," said Dick in the darkened room, "there goes Keino past the pack . . . and now the rest of you start to move around. Okay, now here it comes . . . keep your eye carefully on the Pakistani."

I moved alongside him . . . Fordjour coming with me on my shoulder. Suddenly we saw the Pakistani's right elbow shoot out and crash into my midsection. The next moment I was on the ground.

Timmie was shifting in his chair. Not one given to outbursts of emotion, I could see he was seething inside. Now he grew red-faced with rage.

"That was a foul," he said slowly and deliberately but with intensely controlled emotions. "That is definitely a foul! It's clear as can be. Any rule book, any athletic official in the land would say so."

The video was run several more times. Timmie stalked the room like a caged bear. He was livid. "They *have* to reinstate you. According to international rules, that is not just an option—it is their *required* course of action. They *have* to!"

Within a matter of minutes Timmie's coat was on and he headed out door.

"I'm going to the village," he said. "I'm going to find some officials who'll look at this thing. I don't care if it takes me the rest of the night to set something up. This video shows as clear as day what happened and . . . just don't worry. Something has to be done!"

As it turned out, it did take Timmie nearly the rest of the night. We'd seen the video early in the evening, but because of the tight security surrounding the Olympic Village—and in fact the entire Olympic complex—he had great difficulty moving about freely and finding the right people. He became so entangled that by the time certain of the contacts were made, he'd been forced to drag a few officials out of bed. By this time his fighting spirit was fully aroused.

His mission that night also caused him to miss the finals of the basketball competition (starting after midnight for live television broadcast reasons)—a game that proved to be the crowning touch of frustration for our embattled U.S. team. It had come down to the United States against the Soviet Union—a classic confrontation. With seconds left on the clock and the Russians leading by a mere point, American Doug Collins was fouled going up for what could have been the winning basket. The clock read :03 with Collins standing on the line for two free throws.

He hit the first one. Tie game. Then he dropped in the second and the United States led by a point. As the Soviets threw the ball in bounds, their coach was immediately on the court gesturing for a time-out, which was not allowed by the rules. However, one of the referees blew the clock dead at :01. There was a short confusion, then the Soviets threw the ball in. A reckless long shot caromed off the backboard and the game appeared over. The Americans led by a point.

There was pandemonium. A British official without jurisdiction in the game came down out of the stands, insisting that the clock be set back to three seconds and that the Soviets be given the ball. Despite bitter U.S. protests the clock was finally set back to :03, the Soviets threw in the ball, passed downcourt, and unbelievably sunk a desperation shot to win the game by a point. The crowd booed, the Brazilian official refused to sign the score book, and the outraged scorekeeper went on public record as saying it had been a farce of justice. But the final score—in spite of angry appeals—remained the same.

When Timmie finally got back to us later that night, he had news of a mixed blessing.

"I finally managed to get a meeting set up," he said, "at the stadium tomorrow just before the final."

"Does it look promising?" I asked.

Timmie shrugged with an uncertain look. "I would say yes," he

said. "On the basis of the video alone. I mean, once they see it
. . . with their own eyes . . . there's just no way they can't—"

"Yeah," I interrupted, "but their flexibility hasn't really shown
up till now."

"I know," Timmie went on. "And the only two who are going
to be there are the British IOC fellow and the Dutch official."

"Oh no," I exclaimed.

"I'm afraid so. You've got to remember, Jim, these guys are the
two most powerful men in the world in track and field. Their word
is law."

I sighed. The thought of my fate in their hands was not a pleasant one.

"And," Timmie went on, "they agreed to look at this video only
on the condition that they would be allowed to pass along their final
judgment free from the interfering eyes of their accuser. In other
words, they won't let you into the room with us."

"But there can't be protocol for such a thing," I said. "That's just
going to make a denial all the easier for them."

"I know, Jim, but it's the only way they would consent to view
the film."

The following morning, in a mental state of complete disarray,
I suited up, hoping against hope that maybe I'd still wind up on the
starting line for the final. Timmie went to the stadium, where ABC
had made their booth available for the screening, while I went to
the warm-up track and began to stretch and jog.

Timmie headed confidently to the meeting. He'd checked the
rules to make sure of his position. He'd confirmed that under the
conditions of a foul, an athlete could be waived into the next round
of competition. He was certain I'd be reinstated.

At the warm-up track I jogged . . . and waited. Before long I saw
Timmie walking slowly toward me from the stadium.

"They denied it again, Jim. I'm sorry. They wouldn't look at the
film. In fact, I never even got there. The meeting was cancelled. I
never had the chance to show them the foul."

Dejected, I was speechless.

"They said they would view the video footage one hour *after* the
closing ceremonies, but not before. It would be too controversial,
they said."

It was over. There would be no final 1500-meter race for Jim
Ryun.

(True to their word, the Olympic officials did consent to view the German network footage after the Games were over. The lights were dimmed and Timmie began showing the film. After but a few seconds of the race, one of the officials stood up quickly and ordered that the projector be stopped. He then turned to Timmie with hostility. "Young man," he said, "is this all you've got?"

"Yes," said Timmie.

"We've already seen a film of this race. You've deceived us. You got us here under false pretences. You've got nothing!"

"But if I could just show you where the foul took place," insisted Timmie. "I'm sure that once it's pointed out to you you'll—"

"There is no additional information here," the official replied. "This viewing session is over.")

The media was poised and ready, watching us for any possible news. Graciously, they kept at a distance for a few minutes, allowing Timmie and me the privacy they sensed we needed.

Soon Howard Cosell walked over, accompanied by a cameraman. Others gathered around. Aware of my anguish, Howard was soft-spoken, sympathetic, and very courteous. Eventually the question came, "Jim, what are you going to do now?"

"Well, Howard," I answered slowly, "the first thing I'm going to do is go home with my wife, sit down, and pray about what the Lord wants us to do. After that, I don't know. One thing for sure is I'll never run again as an amateur."

"I realize it's been a devastating week here for all our athletes. But let me get this straight . . . are you talking about turning professional?" asked Howard in the tone that is so uniquely him.

"There've been offers," I replied, "and I have bills to pay. After this there's no need to play the amateur game. I have a family to care for."

I talked with Howard and other reporters for a few minutes more and finally turned away.

The final of the 1500-meter came and went.

Disconsolate, Anne and I walked slowly out of the stadium together. Toward what . . . we did not yet know.

Track & Field News later reported my heat blow by blow:

In his qualifying heat, Ryun stayed near the rear. . . .
With about 550 meters to go . . . he tried to go between two runners. But as later viewing of videotape appeared to indicate . . . a tiring

Mohamed Younis of Pakistan—the leader until 900 meters—swung very wide coming into the straight. He appeared to move into Ryun, perhaps hitting him in the torso with his arm. Ryun then stumbled backwards into Billy Fordjour of Ghana and both went down. As they fell, Fordjour's knee struck Ryun's throat and jaw. Ryun was partially stunned and he suffered a contusion of the Adam's apple. He fell on the curb and injured his hip, scraped his right knee, and sprained his left ankle. Fordjour fell across Ryun's legs, and the world-record holder lay on his back perfectly still . . . as his opponents raced away from him and his Olympic chances ended. . . .

With the field more than 100 yards ahead, Ryun wobbled to his feet and hobbled a few slow steps, holding his hip. Then suddenly he burst into a fast run. People cheered fervently, but the cheers gradually subsided as they realized he had no chance. Ryun himself finally slowed and crossed the finish line. . . .

He was met by his old rival Kip Keino, who patted Ryun's shoulder in sympathy . . . the crowd was unusually silent. . . .

Two days later, Ryun sat . . . and watched Pekka Vasala beat Keino in the homestretch. . . .

The Jim Ryun story had ended. [*Track & Field News,* September 1972]

CHAPTER 17

Professional Track

The public and press were hard put to deal with my Munich performance. They'd primed themselves for a Jim Ryun gold medal. Now, after the headline reports of my fall, the time had clearly come to put the battle-scarred Jim Ryun saga to rest—for good. Many felt I'd again shamed our country and let me know it. Others expressed sympathy, as if I'd died.

Jim Ryun's career is remembered with disappointment. . . . When he fell, we wrapped the Jim Ryun story into a convenient package. His last chance for a gold medal ended pitifully, almost as if prophesied, with a tumble to the track in a 1500-meter heat of the 1972 Munich Olympics. Our softer hearts felt for him. The hard ones filed him away as a loser. [*Philadelphia Daily News,* August 31, 1982]

And the evaluation as to "why?" continued.

In recent times, probably no athlete has been the subject of as much psychoanalysis in the public press as has Jim Ryun. For just about every typewriter-carrying, Freudian sportswriter meeting a deadline, there's a theory as to the inner workings of the mile world-record holder's psyche. Some say Ryun faced too much pressure at too young an age in his track career. Others contend that the twenty-five-year-old Kansas grad has an "athletic death wish." [*Track & Field News,* December 1972]

Because of my sensitive nature it was impossible for me to ignore the disgrace I'd fallen into. For years I'd faced the insatiable public appetite to understand my inner self, my thoughts, my fears, in order to explain why I couldn't "win the big one." Now the whole puzzle of "what happened to Jim Ryun?" became magnified even further. There was simply no way I could steel myself to ignore the hundreds of ways that question subtly bombarded me. I read the papers and books and magazines. I read that my career was "shot," that my "glory, fame, and invincibility were fading," that in reality my "inner psyche hated track." I read that Jim Ryun "brooded about the fragility of his fame," and that I was "star-crossed." I listened to the interviewer's question: "Jim, what happened? Will you run again . . . Is there a Ryun jinx . . . What are your plans . . . what about another crack at 3:50 . . . Is Jim Ryun washed up?" I listened to the boos of the crowd in coming years if my efforts didn't please them.

I never really was concerned about my "glory and invincibility." And I certainly never "brooded about the fragility of my fame." That's the one thing I would have wished for above all else, that my fame *had* been less. But the point is, all this media speculation swirling around with me at its center added greatly to my confused, embittered, "fragile," and frustrated state of mind. After Munich it was unbearable, because now there was no hope, nothing to look forward to, no potential exoneration awaiting me on the victory stand with the gold medal around my neck.

Of course I hadn't really failed. Time eventually clears away the pain and reveals things with greater perspective. But at the time such was my reaction.

Anne and I had become Christians several months prior to the Munich Games. We were very sincere in our early attempts to live a different kind of life and could sense that a change had occurred within us. We had a peace within—what the Bible speaks of as "peace that passes all understanding." Nevertheless, the Munich experience practically destroyed me. As a Christian I tried to respond in my heart as I thought I should, but when I faced myself honestly I knew that I was bitterly angry at the treatment I'd received. I wanted nothing more than to meet that Olympic official one-on-one in an empty room. Because if I'd had the chance, my one desire in life was to deck him good! The resentment nearly consumed me.

Had Anne not stood with me and supported me and had we not been Christians, I feel the skirmish going on inside me would have erupted into a full-scale war. As it was, the battle raged on for some time. I labored in prayer over the animosity I harbored in my heart. Yet being a Christian only intensified the struggle all the more because I knew Christians weren't supposed to feel those sorts of things. Christians were supposed to be loving and peaceful and

Running indoors on the ITA tour was sometimes a
solo effort.

forgiving—right? Yet I certainly wasn't. What I didn't know then
was that it takes time; there's a process of letting go of oneself and
letting God have His way.

Though I continued to run, my caustic attitude soured me toward the whole sport, especially the amateur side of it, whose
leadership I now viewed as hypocritical, to put it mildly. There was
a period when I had a difficult time picking up a copy of *Runner's
World* or *Track & Field News* without feeling a resurgence of the
bitterness toward what had happened in Germany.

Thus there was a great perplexity I felt as a Christian. God had
become a factor in our lives, but for the next several years we didn't
learn about applying the Bible's principles to our daily life-style.
We didn't realize how badly we needed to get together with other
Christians in a more personal environment than church—to have

Bible study, to pray for one another, to encourage and be encouraged through this rough and bumpy time. We simply didn't know enough about being Christians to work very many changes into our life-style or attitudes.

Almost immediately after our return from Munich I signed with the newly formed professional track circuit. I attended a news conference in New York to announce the formation of ITA. The initial bonus allowed us to make a down payment on a house in Santa Barbara that we never would have been able to do otherwise. But over the next three years running with ITA, I only made enough to barely support us.

Our first season opened in Pocatello, Idaho, just two days after our twin sons, Ned and Drew, were born. I'd been slated for a highly publicized special solo 1500 meters that was billed as a record attempt—at 4,500 feet no less! Realizing how laughably absurd this was, I nevertheless complied. Of course, I came nowhere close. It was the first run of the indoor season—in March. I don't recall my time but doubt it was under a 4:05 pace. The crowd loved it, however. I earned $500 for first place (I was the only competitor), and ITA was off and running. (Prize money was $500 for first place, $250 for second, $150 for third, and $50 for fourth.)

Throughout the next four years, ITA attracted an impressive roster of stars. Some joined the second year, others the third. The management negotiated constantly to bring in new blood. Among those who participated were Bob Seagren, Randy Matson, Lee Evans, John Carlos, Steve Smith, Vince Matthews, Dave Wottle, Kip Keino, Ben Jipcho, Bob Hayes, Brian Oldfield, Wyomia Tyus, Mel Pender, Barbara Ferrell, George Young, Gerry Lindgren, Larry James, Tom Von Ruden, Sam Bair, Conrad Nightingale, and Jim Hines. Steve Prefontaine was rumored close to signing before his death. In addition to the prize money, at each season's end a bonus of approximately $2,500 was awarded the athlete in each category with the best overall record.

There was scarcely big money to be made, but we hoped ITA would break open the amateurism problem that had locked up track and field in this country for so long. All of us who participated had high hopes.

But as in most new enterprises, financial difficulties crept in. A number of athletes began to squabble for higher prize money, more expenses, a pension plan, and so on. The simple facts were that there

Following a professional race against Keino, in Kansas City, Missouri.

was not much money in ITA's coffers. Though we ran to a packed 17,000 in Madison Square Garden, we also ran before crowds of 1,000. When ITA ultimately folded in 1976, its founders faced several hundred thousand dollars in debts. The dissension over money represented one of the chief factors causing friction between a vocal minority of athletes and management. This led in turn to disputes about the different viewpoints among the athletes themselves, and ultimately these schisms became unrepairable. The money simply wasn't there.

I look back on these as good years. Though the travel was extremely taxing, quality workouts were almost impossible on a regular basis, and my times were therefore mediocre, I nevertheless felt liberated from the intense scrutiny of my every breath that had characterized my life from 1965 to 1972. My personal emotions and attitudes gradually brightened. With some of the pressure abated, I began to enjoy meeting and talking with people. A few articles even appeared about the "new Jim Ryun," so shocked were reporters on occasion to find me downright talkative, even appearing to enjoy myself in front of the microphones!

On the whole, I felt ITA's management did extremely well considering the odds against them. But the cloud of amateurism pre-

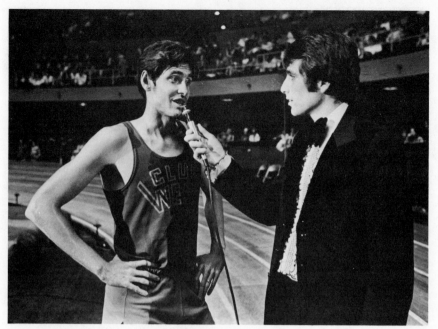

Being interviewed by Marty Liquori.

vented ITA from growing and expanding. Most of us, stars though we had once been, were by then in the twilight of our athletic careers. We attracted people for a time, but newness was constantly needed. Yet it was impossible for ITA to attract quality athletes out of college because they were so concerned with preserving their so-called amateur status in order to make national and Olympic teams. Furthermore, many found they could command larger sums under the table as amateurs than they would have made with ITA as professionals. Three to five thousand dollars was small potatoes for a top-class amateur for a single performance, but he could run a whole year for ITA and not make that much on the tour.

During my involvement with ITA, one of the most touching moments for me personally came when Ben Jipcho approached me with something clearly on his mind. Very simply, he apologized for what he'd done in Mexico City.

I was speechless and moved by the compassion I could sense in his voice.

"I was pressured into it," he said. " 'This is Keino's Olympics,' they told me. 'You must help him. You'll have your day another time.'"

He and I had a deep, mutual respect for one another and had grown friendly on the tour. But this was the first time the subject of Mexico City had arisen between us.

"That's really nice of you to say, Ben," I said, still somewhat taken aback, "but really, I—"

"I'm not just trying to be polite," he interrupted with emotion clearly in his tone. "I really mean it. It was not a fair competition. I went into it knowing I had to be Keino's rabbit and that's simply not right in the Olympic Games. It's contrary to the whole spirit of it."

"I appreciate that," I said. "But I ran a good race and so did Kip. I bear no one any ill because of what happened. I'd have been happy with a third, or even a fifth place, in that race, given the effort I made."

"But I know it was hard for you," he went on. "The press branded you a loser after that and I regret what happened."

"Losing wasn't so bad. It's that few people fully understood Mexico City. It's always nice to talk with someone like you who knew what was really going on. But you don't have to worry about me."

"Nevertheless," the talkative Jipcho went on, "I've never felt right about it since. That was the first time he ever beat you. You were better than all of us and under equitable conditions he never would have then. You were cheated out of a fair shot at the gold medal . . . I think you should have won."

Deeply moved, I thanked him again. And, as I thanked him, memories flashed through my mind of both the 1968 and 1972 Olympics, and I realized how God had in fact begun his wonderful healing within me over the bitterness of those experiences.

As a promotional representative for ITA, I made advance visits to nearly every city on our schedule. For sixteen meets, this added up to about thirty-two trips out of town within a five-month-period. It seemed I was always on the road. There was little time for quality workouts or for my family, and my performances were subpar, usually between 4:00 and 4:08 for an indoor mile.

Underlying the whole period there remained—hidden from view—within me the consuming goal that running represented. My subconscious attitude remained totally absorbed in it. I'd been around this path of making running an idol so many times before, you're going to think I was a pretty obstinate guy not having van-

quished it by now. You're right—I was obstinate. I couldn't shake
the illusion that I had to regain my position as the world's premier
miler in order to gain my self-respect. When added to the smolder-
ing embers of my resentment over Munich and the drudgery of such
mediocre professional performances, many of the same old frustrations continued to haunt me.

I had found peace with God. But I had not yet found peace with
myself.

CHAPTER 18

Saved but Stalled

Growth as a Christian progressed very slowly for me during this period. My natural caution and reserve kept me holding back my true inner self. Coupled with a total devastation over the Olympics, my life seemed to stand still. At the same time, I had to keep going —to continue living.

So it was with this intent—to keep my life going—that I agreed to attend a home Bible study. At a potluck prior to the study, a young man I was vaguely acquainted with walked up and bluntly and innocently addressed me: "Well, Jim, what is Jesus doing in your life?"

I stared blankly back, hemmed and hawed a little, and mumbled some commonplace trivialities. I was annoyed that the guy would have the nerve to embarrass me like that.

In the meantime Anne stood off to the side with her mouth closed, smiling and thinking, "This ought to be good, God. What *are* you doing in his life?"

But I had no answer. I honestly didn't think God was doing anything in me. My faith was dry and my Christian walk stuck in neutral. I had invited Jesus into my life, but I was stalled as far as developing an ongoing relationship of trust with him. I really felt God had let me down—after I had tried so hard and now there was no gold medal. I still loved Him, but in a very distant way.

Throughout the period between 1972 and 1975 I basically stood on the sidelines. Anne attended Bible studies, read books, and was beginning to move forward as a Christian. I was still holding back, hesitant to jump in with both feet. I would quiz Anne after she returned from a Bible study or prayer meeting, and I occasionally read Christian books and prayed. I wanted to behave as a Christian, but there was a reluctance at the same time—a fear of crossing what I had been taught as a child. I still held on to my running career as a security blanket, even an idol. So I might listen to a discussion on spiritual things, but I would be sure not to get involved in the conversation myself. I didn't want it to become too personal. I didn't want to let go of my pride.

But the Lord gradually zeroed in on me.

One by one people came into our lives who pressed my back to the wall and forced me to take a hard look at the reality of my spiritual condition. All these years I had taken such good care of my physical and mental condition, but the third dimension to every human being—my spiritual condition—was in a phase of malnutrition. Although I knew a man eats three meals a day and exercises to keep fit, I couldn't make the correlation of keeping fit spiritually. I was content to watch the children while Anne went to some church function or Bible study. I was content to let her carry on the spiritual dimension of life, even to teach the children Bible stories and prayers. All I wanted was to sit in front of the television, eat my milk and cookies, and go to bed. All the while God sent circumstances my way to get my attention and confront me with the necessity of giving more of my life to Him.

One day, as I sat pondering my fate, my listlessness, and my discouragement, I flashed back to a moment of great significance. It was immediately after the 1972 Olympics when Anne and I were flying to Copenhagen. In nearby Malmo we had previously seen some furniture in a little shop that we were very taken with. We wanted to buy it and have it shipped home. There had been the usual difficulties with the language barrier. Added to this was the shipping problem, our tight schedule, and our limited funds, and we simply didn't know if we would be able to pull it off. So on the plane we were talking about it, wondering what to do.

I happened to notice that the man sitting on the other side of Anne was reading a newspaper in English.

I whispered quietly to Anne, "That man obviously speaks English. Why don't you ask him if he knows a good way to ship some items to the States."

So Anne, friendly conversationalist that she is, turned to him and asked exactly that.

"Sure," he answered in perfect English. "What is it you want to ship?"

We told him all about the furniture we had seen.

"That should be no great problem," he said. "Why don't you tell me exactly what it is you want and where it is. My wife can meet you at the store and have it sent directly to your home. Then once it has arrived, you can send me a check for the charges."

Naturally I was speechless. I thought my hearing had failed me. Here was a perfect stranger offering to take on this sizable task himself, pay for the shipping out of his own pocket, trusting us entirely.

"This man is really different," I thought to myself. "Something about him is unique!"

Having taken care of the furniture business, we introduced ourselves to one another. It was not long before I found out what set him apart. It was the same thing that had drawn me to so many other "unique" persons—he was a Christian. As we continued to talk and visit on the plane, we discovered that this man served as Billy Graham's interpreter for his Swedish crusades.

It was through such "chance" encounters over the years that the Lord kept showing me, "You see, Jim. My people are all around. Whenever people yield themselves to Me, I am faithful. My Spirit inside their hearts sets them apart. They are distinctive because they are full of My life. And as you give yourself more thoroughly to Me as well, I will fill you with more and more of My life. And, Jim, you can trust Me to take care of you and meet your needs, just as I have in this instance through My servant, a total stranger to you. Neither of you are strangers to Me. You are both in My family."

It was during a later conversation that this man made a statement I will never forget. For his words truly were prophetic. He said, "You know, Jim, your fall in Munich was devastating at the time. But the Lord will use that fall for His greater glory. You can be sure of it!"

It was instances like this along the way that would cause me to realize "there's more to life than running." More and more it gradually became clear that if God was who He said He was, then He would care for me. He would fill me with His life, not just the mediocre life I'd been living, but life *full* to overflowing with His provision. These realizations came very slowly. I stubbornly wanted to hold on to the reins of my life.

So far Anne had pretty much run our household, disciplined the children, and so on. Anne was more forceful and I was more reserved; this was the natural pattern that developed between us.

It was during this time of great indecision that Anne's sister Cate came for a visit. She had been a Christian longer than we and was able to see that we were not growing as a Christian couple.

Gently, yet with a firm confidence, she would say to me: "Jim, God has a plan for you. He wants you to be the high priest and leader in your family. He desires that your home be spiritually in order and that there be peace and harmony here. He wants you to lead and sacrifice for your wife and children."

Sometimes I could do nothing more than sheepishly sit there, having no idea what to say. And as difficult as her words were to listen to, they became instrumental in forcing us into some necessary evaluation. She was right. What she was saying came straight from the Bible. Our home *wasn't* ordered as God's word instructs. I *was* neglecting my responsibility as a Christian man, and I *wasn't* growing as I should. But even knowing this, I was still uncomfortable. I didn't like what was going to have to happen to make the changes.

However, seeds were being sown that the Lord would later use. I recall one night in particular. Cate and Anne were in the living room, carrying on one of their enthusiastic discussions about a particular piece of scripture. I had been working in my office nearby and, hearing the voices get louder and louder, I stuck my head through the door and listened for a while. (I didn't actually go *inside* the room or show any signs of wanting to sit down, of course. I knew if I did, they would involve *me* in the discussion!) I merely listened—for quite some time. Because I was curious, I was gradually coming to see that living as a Christian meant more than I was doing.

From many angles God would send people into our lives who demanded that we get moving with the Lord. A young neighbor— a high school boy, himself a zealous Christian—would walk over, greet Anne through the kitchen window while she was doing the dishes, and then put to her the most challenging questions: "Well, what did you read in your Bible today? Have you spent your time alone with the Lord today praying? What has the Lord been saying to you lately?"

Our neighbor was pointing us in directions we needed to go. The

Christian life is not stagnant: you have to be growing, moving, progressing in an ever-deepening relationship with the Lord, or else you wither on the vine. That, unfortunately, is what we were in danger of doing. As a young mother, with young children around all the time, Anne had to take her Bible reading and prayer in bits and pieces; I was on the road so much that I scarcely read my Bible at all. But in retrospect, we can see that we were just making excuses for ourselves.

All these people and circumstances and the books we read from time to time stirred us up toward the spiritual growth missing in our lives. It caused a stretching of our experience to put all these spiritual factors into a life-style application.

This period during which my Christian walk was at such a standstill came to a head in 1975. We had just decided to return to Lawrence in order to train for the following year's professional track circuit. We decided to rent our Santa Barbara home. After advertising the house, we couldn't get a renter. Suddenly there seemed to be no demand for our type of house in that price range. Finances were very tight. We had to rent the house in order to make the payment, and the time for our scheduled departure for Kansas was rapidly approaching. We prayed about it but never really stopped long enough to listen to see if the Lord had an answer for us. My basic operating guideline at the time was, "Hey, it's time for such-and-such . . . and where are you God? Let's go, and if you're behind me, please catch up, because I'm moving." I wasn't willing to wait on the Lord. I ran my life on my own timetable.

So as the moment to leave drew closer and closer, and I became more and more impatient. Finally we received a phone call from some people interested in the house. They promised proper care of it in every way and sounded good on the surface. Something inside me was uncomfortable with them and I knew they probably weren't the right people. (Neither of us was at peace about it but I was anxious to get on with my training and I just wasn't going to listen to any little voices down inside telling me to wait patiently. Besides, we had to get to Kansas to get Heather started in kindergarten. Time was of the essence!) So instead of waiting on the Lord, having patience for Him to send the right people to us, I panicked and accepted their offer. We rented them the house and off we drove to Kansas.

My hastiness and my lack of trust in the Lord proved a huge

mistake! It wasn't long before the rent wasn't being paid, and word came that they were destroying the house. We began taking steps to rectify our mistake—we asked the renters to vacate. After what proved to be a great trauma for all of us, they left. That incident completely drained us.

Although the whole thing was an emotional and financial disaster, it served to wake me up to the emptiness of my life as a Christian. I was still very much just doing my own thing. I wasn't listening to God's voice. I wasn't trusting Him to take care of us or meet our needs. I wasn't being a spiritual leader to my wife or my children. And I wasn't growing in my relationship with Him.

I had been a Christian now four years. However, I had been a very slow learner. I had invited God's spirit to live in my heart, but I had not given Him control. I had still retained my *own* plans, my *own* dreams, my *own* desires, and especially my *own* running career, and they were in the forefront of my thinking. I had been vaguely trying to behave as a Christian, but inside many parts of my life remained unsettled.

For twenty-nine years I had been sitting in the driver's seat. I did what I wanted and life revolved around *me.* When things went well, my *self* felt the gratification and rejoiced. When things went badly, I tried to pull myself up by my own bootstraps. When Anne and I were married, our life together revolved around *me* and *my* running career. After Munich I was embittered because of what those men had done to *me.*

Even after I became a Christian in 1972, my hands still firmly gripped the steering wheel. Thus my progress in the Christian life was slow; deep joy and fulfillment were rather scarce. Running had always been my god, and in a sense it continued to be. In the end I finally had to admit that it was an empty chase. Worldly achievements had not brought me happiness. I had prayed for the Lord to come into my life. But all I had done was open the door to let Him inside. I had not as yet really turned my life over to Him. I had not let Him past the foyer into any other rooms of *my* house, so to speak. The Lord is a gentleman. He will not go where we do not invite Him. Thus many aspects of my life and attitudes remained unchanged. I was still vainly trying to recapture my position as a great runner. All the while the bitterness over Munich ate away at me. I could never forgive what had happened as long as my sole preoccupation remained my *own* Munich experiences. But what of those Olympic officials, men obviously hurting inside with their own bitter memories, torn by unseen pressures and fears? Of course I could never consider such factors as long as my *own* life and career were so dominant on my list of priorities. Forgiveness could only emerge from my heart when I put someone *else's* needs ahead of my own.

All the while, during those four years between 1972 and 1976, the Lord stood patiently by, inching closer to the driver's seat of my life, sending circumstances that caused me to question how much fulfillment I was getting from directing the course of my life myself. All the while caring for me, not allowing disaster to strike, protecting me as a shepherd protects his sheep.

Occasionally a thought would drop into my consciousness, such as: "You know you're not really fulfilled. Even though you're a Christian, you know there must be more to life than this. Why won't you move over? Let Jesus have total control of your life. Let Him show you how to put others ahead of yourself. He'll show you how to forgive the men at Munich. Jesus will give you love for that Olympic official. He's simply a man with needs and emotions and hurts just like you. But your *self* is obscuring your vision from seeing him as God sees him. God loves the Olympic official just as much as God loves you."

Those were "heavy" thoughts—too revealing. Instead of yielding, my resistance stiffened.

I wanted to be free from the weight hanging around my neck from those bitter experiences. But forgive him? How could I possibly—I mean . . . love him? "Lord," I thought, "you've got to be kidding!"

But He bided His time.

"And Jim," I could hear Jesus say, "your marriage could be far more than it is. It's a good relationship you and Anne have. You're a good father. But it still centers around *you*. You haven't yet laid down your life for her. You haven't yet made *her* needs and emotions the predominant focus of your attention. You have not loved her with Christ's love. And the children I've given you—you have so much life to give them. I have so much more to offer you! But, Jim . . . you have to step aside or I'll never be able to."

My hands gripped the steering wheel tightly. I held on for dear life.

"Trust Me, Jim," said the Lord. "I love you and I am altogether trustworthy. All you have to do is let loose your grip. There's a world out there I want to give you. But you have to trust Me. You have to let go . . . you must let go."

But I didn't want to let go. Letting go meant a leap into the unknown. It required relinquishing twenty-nine years of defenses I'd built up. It frightened me to contemplate the potentially horrid consequences. What if the Lord called me to the slums of India as a missionary? Or Watts, or Harlem, or required more of me than I could give? What if everyone laughed at me for following a man who had been dead for 1950 years? Or what if He made me give up—of all things—running?

I hung on by a thread, paralyzed at the thought of plunging into the untraveled regions of "trusting God." I knew in my head that Jesus Christ was the way, the truth, and the life. But I began to wonder what I'd gotten myself into. What would become of *me?*

I was like the boy in the story riding his tricycle near a dangerous cliff. Without realizing where he was going, he rode right over the edge and fell into thin air. Fortunately, a few feet over the bank he crashed into the remains of a tree growing horizontally out from the sheer drop of earth and rock. He clutched the scraggly branches for dear life, not daring to glance down, screaming for help.

"Help, help!" he yelled. "Help me—please . . . if anybody's there, help me! Somebody help me!"

The boy's weight strained the tree's roots and it slowly sagged. He knew it would not hold much longer and there was no way he could climb up to safety.

"Help!" he cried out once more. "Can anybody hear me? Help! Is anybody there?"

Suddenly he heard a deep, resounding voice, seemingly out of the sky. "I can help you."

"You can?" said the boy excitedly, looking around. "Where are you?"

"I'm up here, above you. All you have to do is trust me and do as I say."

It was an awesome sound. The boy was nearly as afraid of the voice he couldn't see as he was of the frightful jam he was in. But his options were severely limited.

"Who . . . who are you anyway?" asked the boy cautiously.

"God," the voice echoed, sending a slight tremor through the mountain.

The youngster hesitated a moment, then said, "OOOOOkay . . . what do you want me to do?"

"Let go of the branch," the voice answered back, even more awesomely than before.

There was a pause.

The boy said nothing, obviously thinking over his predicament. After a few moments his high-pitched voice was heard to call out, "Is there anybody *else* out there?"

Well, that's exactly how I felt. Like that prudent lad, I began to realize it would require a leap of commitment like I'd never before faced. If I was going to stick with living as a Christian, I was going to have to begin taking it seriously. Yet I wasn't at all sure I wanted the kind of help God seemed to be offering.

CHAPTER 19

Letting Go

During the 1975 season I began to have difficulty with the Achilles portion of one of my heels. It was a slow-growing problem, but it gradually began to affect both workouts and performances. It became especially painful when running on indoor board tracks, where 90 percent of ITA's racing occurred. After the season was over and I was well rested, I thought I had the problem licked and was anticipating great times the following season. With that in view, we returned to Kansas where I began training with great intensity, excited about my fourth season with ITA. We also began a weekly Bible study with Clara and Bernie, which eventually drew many other hungry, seeking "baby" Christians. I was feeling unsettled in my Christian walk, and by this time Anne was washed out on the whole running scene and wondering how much longer I was going to keep it up.

One night as we were lying in bed, Anne posed the question, "What will you do when the Lord calls you into retirement?" The question seemed somehow prophetic—a question I didn't want to face—at least not yet.

My reply was, "We'll cross that bridge when we come to it."

I wanted a stable position, as does any man with a family. Unless there opened up some viable alternative, I had no intention of just walking away from ITA. It had come to represent my security. I hadn't even stopped to pray about it. I simply was going to keep running, always with the dream of climbing back to the top, and made no real efforts to discover what the Lord's thinking might be in the matter.

The first meet of the 1976 season approached, to be held in Salt Lake City. I was scheduled to run a half-mile. Midway through the race my heel was screaming with such pain that I simply could not take another step. I slowed and dropped out, reminiscent of a recurring bad dream. The discouragement stemmed not so much from having to stop during the race but from the question "Will this foot ever be whole again?"

I called Anne and as we commiserated together on the phone, I said, "You know, honey, I'm prepared to do whatever the Lord wants. If He wants me to retire, I'm ready."

I returned home. Several nights later, as I lay in bed praying before falling asleep, deep within my spirit I heard something distinctly like an audible voice. The Lord said, "You've run a good race, you've fought a good fight. It's finished. I have something more for you."

As I continued to lay there, I began to do something very unusual for me, something I just don't do. I began to weep. It was not from grief or disappointment, but my emotions were being touched on so many levels. It was a final release, the closing of a lengthy chapter of my life. There were happy memories, as well as sad ones. But you always anticipate retiring on a high note. To step off the track because your Achilles tendon is killing you, never to run on the track again—that is just not the way you envision ending your career.

I woke Anne up and said, "Anne . . . I think the Lord just spoke to me." Then I recounted what He'd said.

"Hallelujah!" she shouted.

We promptly jumped out of bed to celebrate. We were so noisy that we woke up Anne's brother Tom, who was staying with us. An emotional dam had broken within each of us; it was difficult to still. Then a soft cloud seemed to settle over us. Strange as it seems at a time such as that, one of us turned on the TV, but I was too immersed in my own thoughts to be more than vaguely aware of it.

Naturally, I was a bit frightened. I had no idea what we would do. But from that moment on I found myself ready to depend on the Lord in a much greater way, letting go of my security and all that running had come to represent for me in order to allow Him to meet our needs and direct the future of our lives. Along with the apprehension came a corresponding exultation. We were jumping into the unknown. Hey, I thought, this is going to be exciting, a real adventure!

As I gradually came back to myself, who should I look up to see staring back at me from the TV but Chuck Colson, a man who had himself known the ups and downs of life. He was sharing very openly on a live network interview about how he had come to know the love of God and the reality of His faithfulness.

God's timing is always beyond our human resources. I sat and listened to Chuck Colson share how God had met him where he was and when he needed Him the most. And at that moment in my life, as I was just beginning a new walk of trust in the Lord, it was exactly the dose of encouragement I needed. God knew that and timed the events to coincide beautifully.

The next day I shared with Timmie what had happened. He listened graciously, if a bit skeptically, and then suggested we call a press conference to make the announcement public.

Several days later the press room at the University of Kansas was filled with about sixty reporters, sitting, standing, literally jammed into the room. I'd stood before so many of these men and women frequently through the years. A certain nostalgia welled up inside me knowing this would likely be the last time.

"I thank you all for coming," I began. "We've been through a lot together these last twelve or thirteen years. There've been many ups and downs, and I just want to say how much I appreciate your kindness toward me. Now I've got something to tell you that will probably sound like a Billy Graham testimony . . ."

I paused, then smiled, ". . . but you're probably starting to get used to that sort of thing from me by now, right?"

There were a few scattered, good-natured laughs lightening the initial heaviness I sensed in the room.

"I know it may sound a bit peculiar, and I don't know how each of you will respond, but I want to lay it out very clearly to you."

I then went on to relate exactly what had happened while I was lying in bed and said it was my firm conviction that the Lord had definitely spoken to me and told me to retire. I told them that His exact words were "You've run a good race, you've fought a good fight. It's finished. I have something more for you."

"So today I am doing just that. I am announcing to you that I am retiring from active competitive running."

Reporters' pencils and note pads and photographers' cameras were actively recording my every word.

I went on to reflect on all the wonderful relationships I had

enjoyed with members of the press through the years—my friendship with photographer Rich Clarkson, the kindness of men such
as Joe McGuff of the *Kansas City Star* and Bob Hensen of the *Topeka
Capital-Journal*. Though I'd suffered through many rocky times because of the constant publicity, this core of local personnel had
always treated me with graciousness and respect, and I thanked
them for their support and encouragement.

"Finally," I said in conclusion, "I want you to know that today
is in no way a sad moment for me. I look back on my career with
a great feeling of accomplishment. I've run for thirteen years. That's
a long time! There've been some notable achievements and I am
proud of this period of my life. But athletes cannot sustain such a
peak forever. The era of my running career is over."

I continued, "I feel great about this decision! I don't know what's
on the horizon for Anne and me, but the other night the Lord said,
'I have other things for you to do.' I must tell you I have no idea
as yet what those things might be. I'm anxious to find out and
eagerly looking forward to the future."

Everyone present listened most courteously and later I was filled
with gratitude to find that for the most part my statements were
printed throughout the country exactly as I had given them (something that hadn't always happened during my career).

Walking out of that press conference signaled a new chapter in
our lives for me and my family. One era had passed, another had
begun. Not just with the running, but spiritually as well. A new
world was before us. As yet we had not the slightest inkling of what
the future held. I had no job, we had no regular income, and with
Catharine's birth the previous summer we now had four young
children to care for—Heather was five, Drew and Ned were three,
and Catharine was eight months old.

Along with the uneasiness about launching into the future with
no source of supply tied down, at the same time there was a sense
of, "Hey . . . wow! Let's watch and see how the Lord is going to
work." We literally did not know what we would be doing two
hours from now, much less the next day.

During the press conference, a number of reporters simply could
not grasp the fact that our future was totally a blank sheet of paper.
After I'd finished my statement, the obvious question was posed:
"Well, that's wonderful. You've stopped running. But now . . . how
are you going to make a livelihood?"

"I really don't know," I answered. "I just don't have an answer for you. But I do know that the God of this universe whom I love and who has already told me what I related to you today has assured me He will provide for my family's needs."

Then I quoted to them from Matthew 6 about God's provision for the birds of the air and the lilies of the field and God's promise that He knows our needs and will provide for us as He does for them. I knew that with God all things are possible. I knew I was trained in a number of areas. I had done a lot of work as a photojournalist. I was not tempting God and saying, "Okay, let's see what you can do now" but rather "Lord, I am willing to let you guide me down this road called life."

Not content with that particular answer, one of the men came back with, "But what are you going to *do* now?"

I simply answered, "Well, we're going to pick Heather up from school, drive to McDonald's and get a hamburger, and then go home."

That was all there was. We had no other plans beyond that.

To a very real extent, my walk of faith with God began that day. Retiring from professional track symbolized my letting go of the branch. I scarcely grasped all the implications immediately, but that process at last enabled me to abdicate my position of "running the show" in favor of one greater than myself. Sure—I was terrified of the unknown. But God had at last stretched me to the point where I was willing to seek the future from a perspective other than how it concerned *me* and *my* running. I let go of my *self* and said, "Okay, Lord, I'll trust *you* for guidance and direction." Somehow we knew the Lord would not let us down."

So as we left the university for McDonald's that day, it really was a major turning point for me personally. It was at that point that my walk with God ceased to be intellectual and became a day-by-day, moment-by-moment dependence on Him. He knew our needs and would provide them. There was a great peace Anne and I felt in knowing we were out there with nothing to fall back on, utterly trusting Him to get us from one day to the next.

It was a life-style I'd never experienced before. I had always been taught—by my parents, in school, and by Coach Timmons—that you plan for the rainy day, you set goals, you mark out the direction of your life in advance. This leap into midair was contrary to all that.

Driving through Lawrence after the press conference, Anne and I both felt a great release in our spirits. A weight had been lifted from my shoulders.

"Wow . . . it's done!" I exclaimed. "I have actually retired from running. I can hardly believe it."

"Praise the Lord!" said Anne.

"Amen!"

"You've been at it thirteen years."

"A long time," I said. "Almost half my entire life."

"Jim," said Anne quietly, "is there any . . . I mean, are you sad? Any regrets about today?"

I thought for a moment, then answered, "I guess a part of me always wishes things might have been different. But I feel so free! Really for the first time I can remember. It's as though someone had clipped the ties and let me loose."

"I sense that, too," said Anne, "that today is a new start for us."

"A grand adventure that's just beginning!"

"It's like our lives have been dormant for a long time and are about to blossom."

"Lord," I prayed aloud right as we drove, "thank you for this day of beginnings. We put ourselves totally in your hands. We are willing to go anywhere, do anything, speak to anyone—from this day on. Our lives are yours."

"*You* are steering our course, Jesus," prayed Anne. "And we thank you and give you our praise."

We had let go of the branch and were sailing through midair. We both had such a sense of peace that we were doing the right thing because we were in His hands.

"Well, Lord," we wondered, "what's next?"

CHAPTER 20

New Steps

The impact of the giant leap of faith that retirement represented was immediate. The consequences of trusting God more totally began to surface and our lives at once took off in many new directions of growth.

Within just three or four weeks I found myself, along with Anne, attending a week-long seminar on Christian family living. Another couple, who felt this to be something very important for us, had invited us and paid our way, and then they actually took us to the meetings and accompanied us through it.

It was a first for me—stepping out, going to a crusade, attending a large public meeting of that kind, submitting myself to an outside teaching that wasn't "church" sanctioned. Inside me was a fear that if I went to this thing, it would be like an evangelistic crusade where I would be put on the spot. I had been walking so cautiously and hesitantly as a Christian, always in mortal terror that someone would ask me a question I couldn't answer, make me go forward, or ask me to give my "testimony." So as we prepared for the series of meetings there was a certain uneasy, queasy feeling that I might be confronted as I had been at the potluck.

But there was a difference now.

At last God *was* doing something in my life! Turning myself over to Him, stepping aside and giving Him control, and relinquishing my own goals and plans for life allowed the Lord to get on with what had been His intention all along—the remaking of Jim Ryun into the image of His Son. That is, of course, His intention with us all. But we are so stubborn, so reluctant to permit Him to do the very work for which He created us.

Therefore many of my old preretirement anxieties caused me to get out of the car in the huge parking lot and walk toward the building that first Monday evening a bit squeamishly. As we entered the old Kansas City Municipal Auditorium, I was in for a surprise. The whole atmosphere was so upbeat and cheerful. People were friendly and smiling, obviously excited to be there and eager to be taught. There were no pews and robes, no somber organ music and long faces.

"Hey," I thought to myself, "this is more like a concert than a church service! It's not going to be so bad after all."

I drank it in. It wasn't threatening in the least and the premonition of how discomforting it might be was quickly dispelled.

As evidence that my life was now on a different footing, when it came time for us to register, under "Job Occupation" I wrote, "Free-lancing for the Lord." At the time I thought I was being sincere, although now it seems rather a brash statement to make. At the same time it did rather accurately express our desire to be open and available for God in new ways.

As the week of meetings progressed, I sat there and heard things that were completely foreign to my way of life. The seminar leader was not just making some "recommendations" or spouting off about his personal views and biases. He stated very clearly, "These are the Biblical patterns . . . if you're living differently than this, then you're living in opposition to what God clearly instructs."

It was abundantly clear that at about every point I had indeed *not* been patterning my life according to God's principles. In the seminar we were told that husbands are to be the authority, the high priest in their families—leading their wives, taking charge of raising their children, through love and sacrifice. This, however, represented the exact opposite of how Anne and I had been raising our family.

These teachings jolted me. I realized, "This is completely contrary to how we have been operating in our home."

Then Cate's timely words rushed back out of my memory: "What's the matter, Jim? Don't you realize you get to be the high priest in your home? It's a privilege given you by God."

The seminar leader taught the Biblical principle of the tithe, that 10 percent of everything belongs to God. "But not," he stressed emphatically, "*after* you've taken out all your expenses and deductions. The 10 percent tithe is right off the top, the very first thing that comes out of your paycheck!"

Now I was really squirming in my seat on the bleachers of that auditorium. Because next to running, money had for years been my most pressing worry. I always had to have things completely taken care of and planned out in advance. My view on church collections was if I put in a dollar bill, where did I go to get change?

So these tenets represented revolutionary concepts for me, especially in that right then—as we sat there listening—we had no income and were flat broke. "Give me a break," I thought, "How can I possibly tithe when I don't have any money?"

But the seminar leader wasn't through with me yet. Next he went on to discuss the necessity of waiting for God, trusting Him patiently. If He has given a promise, then your responsibility is to allow Him to implement it. He will bring it about in His timing and in His own way. He will always prove faithful if we patiently sit back and trust Him. The leader cited the example from the book of Genesis where God promised that Abraham would have a son who would be the father of a great nation. In impatience Abraham took matters into his own hands. Thus out of his untrusting relationship with Hagar came an illegitimate son who fathered the Arab nations and brought 4,000 years of strife and bloodshed into the world. Abraham's impatience cost a heavy price.

Suddenly the painful memory rushed back into my mind of the horrible scrape I had gotten us into when renting our Santa Barbara home—all because of my impatience. I had not waited patiently for the Lord. I had gone charging off full steam ahead on my own, not trusting God to take care of the situation. Like Abraham, my independence cost us a great deal of strife.

By this time—through the speaker—God really had my attention!

Everything had been stripped away—my running career, the house in Santa Barbara, financial security, a steady job. It was all gone!

Retiring from the pro track circuit represented a crossroads moment in our lives. The seminar proved to be the springboard into new areas of growth as we fully dedicated ourselves to an alternative way of life. The seminar leader's words had both convicted me of my own selfish and sinful attitudes, while at the same time stimulating me and challenging me to change many past patterns.

Thus we began taking God's principles far more seriously and practically than we had in the past. Through this we began to apprehend more clearly that the key to spiritual life and vitality is *living* God's principles, not merely knowing about them. That is what produces an abundant and fulfilled life. The Christian life is one of obedience to God and trusting Him, not a life of study and knowledge about God.

Therefore, Anne and I now found ourselves regularly sitting down at the kitchen table in the evenings after the children were in bed, with our Bibles open before us. We would read a portion of Scripture and then talk about it . . . and talk about it . . . and talk about it! Digesting it, asking questions, bouncing ideas off one another. (A total and complete detailed openness and honesty had always been a primary ingredient in our relationship together.) Whenever we discussed Scripture in the past, I would usually find a way to argue around what was being said, trying to evade this or that part of it. That is the approach to Scripture I had been taught in church as a child—yes, it says this, but really we know it means something else.

Now I was at last ready to jump into my walk with the Lord with both feet. Therefore, following Anne's example and encouragement, we were responding, "That's what it says. We believe it. Let's do it!"

So we sat by the hour discussing what a particular segment of Scripture might mean. Not in order to increase our head knowledge but rather so that we could learn how to apply its principles in our daily life experiences. We became serious not only about learning what the Bible said but about doing it as well.

I gradually took a more active role in the family, making decisions I might have previously shrugged off. I made a concerted effort to pray every day that God would enable me to be the "high priest," a godly leader to my wife and children. And I certainly needed God's help! Because if there's anything I'm not by natural personality, it's a leader. Yet God had challenged me—through Cate and the seminar leader and His Word—that such was my role and my responsibility as a man of God. Therefore, living with God was not an option but rather a privilege. I had to make that a serious personal priority—whether it came naturally or not. I found that God's most natural way, the way He meant all of us to live in the very beginning, was under His Lordship.

On the other side of the coin, Anne found herself challenged to take a more joint role with me instead of moving off independently on her own as we had both been content for her to do in the past. Ordinarily we thoroughly discussed anything that came up in a total atmosphere of equality. Now we both had to make huge adjustments once the discussion phase was over: Anne had to learn to sit back, even passively at times, and yield to my leadership; all the while I had to learn to summon the guts to step out and assert myself with a firm decision. That was hard!

It was especially hard because our personalities were naturally bent in the opposite directions. We made diligent efforts to retrain ourselves because we could clearly see that the Biblical teaching concerning God's ordained order for families was founded on a husband's leadership. Both of us would have preferred for things to remain as they had been. But if we intended to take the Bible seriously—which we did—and wanted to pattern our lives after it —which we did—then we had to do what it said. And we did so willingly, knowing God's ways had been tested and proven true in so many other marriages. We wanted the best there was and knew God held the answer. After all, we had found Jesus to be the answer to that nagging question "What is life all about?" and weren't about to let it slip away because of our resistent, unyielding personalities.

There arose an incident that graphically illustrated this change. I had a photographic assignment that entailed a trip of several days to San Francisco, where another of Anne's sisters, Susan, lived. Anne was excited about going with me, had the bags all packed, the children readied, and was enthusiastically anticipating a few days with her sister in the city. However, the whole purpose of the trip rested on my receiving certain camera equipment before we left on Friday.

All week we waited and it did not come. I was certain it would arrive on Thursday. But when the UPS man came, there was no such package.

Well . . . Friday, there was no question it would arrive. So we loaded up our Buick station wagon, the children got all packed and ready with coloring books, Christian story tapes, playpen, and so on. We were still excited and anticipating leaving any moment.

When the time for the UPS delivery came, the van drove right past our house. I couldn't believe it!

I went to the phone and dialed the UPS warehouse.

"Are you sure there's no package for me?" I asked. "Could it have been overlooked or come in after the delivery van was sent out?"

"No," they said after a thorough search. "There's just no package."

Slowly I walked outside where Anne and the children were playing on the swing set, ready to hop in the car and take off. I sat down on one of the swings beside Anne and simply said, "We're not going."

In her mind Anne was thinking, "Well . . . why can't we go anyway? So what if the package didn't come? We can still take a trip, have some fun."

Anne knew that if she kicked up enough of a fuss and forced the issue, I would probably have given in. Instead she simply responded, "Oh . . . okay."

It proved a significant moment for both of us. It took a determined step of obedience toward the role for which I knew God was preparing me for me to make such an assertive decision. And it took great humility and self-control on Anne's part to submit to a decision she didn't like.

There was a great peace in both our hearts because we were learning to function harmoniously according to the scriptural pattern. Such moments, far from driving us apart, deepened our love for one another and strengthened our capacity to discuss, negotiate, and mutually work things out for the best for the whole family.

More and more, again with Anne's help, encouragement, and support, I found myself taking a more active role with the children —disciplining them, reading to them, playing with them, incorporating them occasionally into my travel. Whereas previously Sunday had been a day to do nothing but turn on the football game and sit there all day (I was a television addict), now we began to be more creative in how we used our time as a family. For a period we boxed up the television and took it out to the garage. We spent more hours reading Bible stories, playing family games, taking walks or bike rides. We began nightly family devotions and prayer times. If I was going to the track for a jog or easy run, we would all pile into the car and go together.

At all these points, as I set myself to live by God's principles in one thing, the next one I faced became that much easier. With every succeeding step of obedience I was strengthened for stiffer challenges that would lie ahead. In listening to God's voice regarding retiring, a pattern of growth was made possible and God's leading became clearer and clearer all the time.

But trusting the Lord is never easy!

Finances continued to offer a great challenge to my spiritual fortitude. There was no longer a salary coming in and it required greater faith than I possessed to trust God to meet our needs. It went against my upbringing, my personality, and my manhood. Nevertheless, we found ourselves doing what God called us to do—give. Give of our time, our talents, and, yes, whatever money we had. At one point, we felt impressed (after praying) to give our last $100 to our local church. Wow, what a step of faith that took! Little did we know then that it was in giving that you receive.

About this time there was in Lawrence a group of Christian young people whose vision was to help people in need. They would go to various supermarkets after closing and with permission scrounge the garbage bins for outdated but otherwise edible vegetables and produce. To my knowledge none of them knew specifically of our needs. But God led them upon occasion to tithe their own food to us, and more than once we would discover cardboard boxes on our porch stuffed with food. None of the Ryuns were really that fond of broccoli. But broccoli was given in abundance and broccoli it was—for breakfast in omelettes, for lunch in salads, for dinner as the main staple. Boy, did we come to be thankful for broccoli!

Desiring to take God's principles seriously at every point, not just selectively, we wanted to begin tithing. This was something I really had to wrestle with personally. To give the Lord 10 percent —*right off the top!*—that was hard for me to choke down.

"But God," I argued inside myself, "we have so little already. What if I can't feed my family? Couldn't we maybe start with 2 percent, or maybe 3 percent? does it have to be a full 10 percent?"

Our decision to begin tithing seems a bit hilarious now as I look back because at that particular time we had nothing coming in. There was no income to tithe on!

But the Lord wanted us to give. Not to extract a painful sacrifice from us, but because—in God's economy, which is upside-down from the world's way of looking at things—it is through giving that prosperity comes. He's already promised to take care of our needs 100 percent, so what's a 10 percent return to Him on His investment

202 / IN QUEST OF GOLD

in us? God gives to us in exact proportion as we give ourselves. Therefore the tithe is the door that can open the floodgates of God's abundance into our own lives. The more miserly our giving, the more miserly the blessings God is able to give. He wants *all* of us.

Therefore, the Lord wouldn't let me ignore the need to tithe and kept putting it in my mind, challenging me to let loose of my wallet and give Him dominion of that part of my life too.

My thoughts brought me back to just a few weeks earlier when the Lord had requested our last $100 and how we had mailed it right away—in case of a change of heart. The Lord just would not allow me to weasel out of giving His tithe. He knew our giving that $100 to be the best thing for us—it would open up our lives to the flow of His provision and allow us to trust Him for greater and greater things. To my well-ordered way of life, that was a giant and scary step!

After we sent the $100 check, we wrote down and figured up all the expenses we knew of in the months ahead, all our needs— gas, food, electricity, water, rent, auto payments, insurance, doctor and dental bills, occasional shoes or clothes for the children, and on top of all that the payments on the house back in Santa Barbara that was now vacant.

When we had it all totaled up it seemed like an unbelievable sum of money. Especially since we had a grand sum of $10 in the bank and nothing at all coming in! The situation was ludicrous from a human standpoint.

So there Anne and I sat with all these financial needs written on this piece of paper. It seemed so huge! We thought, "Boy, Lord, you're really going to have to do something here. This is some pickle we're in!"

We laid our hands on that paper and prayed over it and simply asked the Lord—somehow—to meet these needs and to provide for us. We called Bernie and Clara and shared the need with them and they prayed with us again, right then over the phone.

We were learning that impossible circumstances are the Lord's favorite workshop. This proved to be one of the first of many times when we would stand back to see the Lord's hand intervene in a most timely way in response to the tiny steps of faith we were attempting to take.

Within just a few short days of praying that prayer, Post Cereals called to talk with me about being a spokesman for a program they were starting in which box tops were redeemable for playground and sporting equipment. I would be traveling for them almost immediately and our bills during that period of time were completely covered. The Lord was indeed in control and had proved Himself to us of all people!

CHAPTER 21

God Is Faithful

During the period between 1973 and 1981 we conducted running camps throughout the country. When they got underway we simply worked as representatives of Invest West, a company that managed many different types of sports camps. In 1976 we found ourselves wanting the freedom to make the camps Christian in nature and format. After much prayer, we began "Jim Ryun Running Camps."

They proved a major arena that God used to solidify our growth as Christians. Many aspects came into the planning and execution of a week-long camp (usually held on college campuses)—from housing and food and finances to counseling and scheduling and literature—that demanded that we either trust the Lord to pull it off, or fall flat on our faces. All along the way the camps involved our entire family. Anne was a full partner with me in the ministry of it and each of the children interacted and developed relationships with the campers as well. The camps brought into focus many things the Lord had to teach us and forced us to rely on Him, for we did not have the experience or organizational background to do much of what was required.

Money continued to be an area where we went often to the Lord in prayer. The cost of the week for a camper only covered expenses. No profit was made and we did not receive a salary or income from the camps. The counselors who joined us did so as a ministry, as unto the Lord, to help others find out how life was meant to be lived.

I recall one afternoon, walking out onto the patio and thinking about the upcoming camp we were preparing for. There was no extra money in our bank account and we needed fifty campers just to break even on expenses. At this point we only had twenty-five or thirty signed up and the time was getting short. I felt terrible, like a tremendous weight rested on me. God was still dealing with me in the area of leadership. I was very much like Moses in the Old Testament—a reluctant leader, squirming and arguing with God every step of the way: "Can't you get somebody else to do it, God? I'm no leader!" Yet God had somehow chosen me to be the vehicle for this particular ministry, the head and organizer and decision maker. On this particular afternoon I wasn't thinking of the spiritual dimensions of such leadership, but instead about the plain and simple fact that I was also the one who was financially liable if we couldn't meet our expenses. It was *my* head they would be after!

I was thinking about it, evaluating the figures. I totaled it up and I've forgotten how many thousands of dollars we were short at the time, but it was several, and I was plainly uncomfortable.

"Lord," I thought silently, "we've come this far. I know you want these camps to succeed. So we're going to keep going and go the whole way, debts or not. If it means having to sell this house at the end of the summer to make up whatever financial deficits there are, then we will. Because I really feel You've called us to do this."

Out of those few moments of reaffirmed dedication to the Lord and what I sensed He had called me to do, I emerged feeling stronger and confident. It was a small personal victory for me as a Christian and as an emerging man who was learning to take responsibility and move forward with it. There was a peace that came in knowing we were out there on a limb, trusting wholly in God and not some company or fat bank account. There was no one to bail us out except Him. (As it turned out, the Lord brought just the number of campers to the next camp that we needed to break even.)

Out of the prayer that went into every camp's preparation emerged many life-changing experiences and relationships. On our staff we had Christian athletes from all over the world, including Olympians. They would mix with the campers (usually youngsters in their teens, although we had the complete spectrum, including a doctor who was over sixty and Anne's father who himself is a jogger), run with them, share with them. We ran and jogged twice a day, swam, conducted clinics on training, diet, racing, form, techniques, and so on. I showed film clips of some of my old races. We started and ended the day with Bible studies, sensing so dearly the deep need to integrate Jesus and His life-style into everyday living. The camps were highly structured and disciplined and I think that's one of the features the campers responded to so well that made the week so memorable and enjoyable.

Travel to and from the various camps was always interesting and exhausting. In the beginning there was no money for plane fares or anything as extravagant as that. We drove everywhere—from Santa Barbara to Tulsa, Oklahoma to Vancouver, B.C., back to Santa Barbara . . . wherever there was a camp being held. And with us we packed the boxes and boxes of posters, t-shirts, athletic gear, family clothes, paperwork, first aid kit, sports equipment, and typewriter. For any given week there would be forty or fifty separate pieces of luggage. We literally moved home and office to set up camp at the different location.

We often camped along the way, in order to keep expenses to a minimum. I will always remember the one summer we were driving from Southern California to Oklahoma. We had just completed a camp in California and only had the space of a week to drive to Oral Roberts University and get all prepared for the next one. We pulled into a little KOA campground just outside Tucumcari, New Mexico after a long day's drive. We struggled through the ordeal of setting up the tents. We—our family and four counselors—were in two cars and had three small tents between us.

At last ready for night to descend, we drove back into town for dinner at the Pizza Hut. We were all exhausted. Right at the table as we were eating someone said to one of our counselors, Scott Gillis, "Scott, Scott, are you awake?"

He had been sitting there at the table, straight up but sound asleep.

He woke up with a start to gales of laughter and shouted, "I'm awake . . . I'm awake!"

Leaving the Pizza Hut and heading back toward KOA we noticed that a violent summer's storm appeared to be moving into the area. We hurried back and got Heather, Catharine, Ned, and Drew to the bathroom, into their pajamas, and into their sleeping bags. By this time the wind was howling all about. Finally Anne and I jumped into our sleeping bags and tried to settle down for a restful night. We were all crammed in pretty tight, yet there was something cozy about being there, all together as a family in the safety of our tent while the wind was swirling and whistling and the rain was pouring down.

Now if you can get a picture of the sort of tent I'm talking about, you'll understand why my concern grew steadily greater as the wind and rain increased. It was a lightweight nylon tent with those wonderful, light aluminum rods to hold it together. And when the wind blows, it may hold it together in some cases.

In this particular case, a really fierce wind began to blow. About halfway through the night suddenly the sky exploded with brilliant flashes of lightning and deafening claps of thunder and almost immediately torrents of rain poured down.

The wind was still blowing and water flooded into the tent— which by this time had begun to collapse. The children were terrified, all clambering out of their sleeping bags to get to Anne and me for what they hoped would be safety.

"Thank you, Lord, for protecting us," we prayed.

I have to admit that there was a quiver in my voice as I prayed, because it had become really terrifying. I genuinely thought that we might be in the path of an approaching tornado, or that lightening could strike. Anne was rebuking Satan and the storm in Jesus' name while I was trying in vain to keep the crazy tent in one piece.

Gradually, a peacefulness came over us. "The Lord is here," Anne said. "We have no need to fear." Anne had actually seen Jesus in the form of a great light come into the tent and give His peace.

Finally we packed up the kids and swished them into the VW bus. We put the seats down and settled the children as best we could. Then I went back to piece together what was left of the tent, all the rods bent and twisted out of shape and the pieces of nylon flapping and blowing in the wind. I knew morning would eventually come.

After packing up that next morning, we were all in one accord chorusing "Tulsa tonight."

And drive we did—straight through. We were eager to get this pilgrimage over with! As we drove through Amarillo, the temperature read 105° on the local bank clock. That gave us even more incentive to continue on. By the time we arrived and began the set-up procedures for the camp, you can imagine what we felt like physically.

There is something sustaining about being involved in a ministry for the Lord, and He adds to physical strength with an extra dose of His Spirit.

Throughout those years, first taking little baby steps of trying God's principles, then gradually growing in confidence as we walked more intimately with Him, life took on new brightness and depth. The years following retirement became distinctively new. As Anne and I committed more and more of the details of life to the Lord, He more and more carried out a transformation within us— a process of making us more Christ-like in our attitudes and outlook, a process that continues to this day and will continue until He comes back again. Gradually I came to see that this rich quality of life the Lord gives—the smile on one's face and the joy in one's heart —can never come about as a result of worldly success, whether it be gold medals or wealth or great power. In my life the only way the Lord was able to get me to the point of turning myself totally over to Him was to take away the petty tokens of worldly acclaim I was seeking. Since running had been my one and only god, in order to give me something far better and more enduring, He had to take my substitute god away. Thus I grew to a point of genuine thankfulness for what happened that day on the Munich track in 1972. For out of the dust of defeat blossomed the new life that came to flourish in my heart. Finally, I am always quick to recall the words of my Swedish friend, "God will use the fall for His glory," and I realize He has done precisely that.

What do I do when painful circumstances come my way? That's what separates the significant life from the commonplace. It's easy to bask in the adulation. But getting up and moving on in the face of failure . . . that's another matter. That takes guts. That's where maturity and strength of character come from. Not from the good times, but from the hard ones. Fortitude is born during adversity, not during success. I hadn't done too well in adopting this attitude through the years. But finally the Lord was getting through.

"Thank you, Jesus," I began to say at last. "Thank you for allowing me to experience life through all its ups and downs, as you yourself did when you were on earth. Thank you, for standing by me through it all."

This new attitude emancipated me to grow and broaden into previously unexplored avenues of life. I rejoiced at last to say, "Lord, I forgive them, all those Olympic officials whom I have had such bitterness towards. Forgive me, Lord, for holding on to those feelings that are in direct contrast to you, to your love. Help me to see them as you see them—your creations whom you love."

As a normal outgrowth of the deeper dimensions of our Christian experience came the desire to share the Lord's love with those we met. The Lord gradually replaced my previous reticence with a great love for people and enthusiasm to share with them and get to know them. Simply put, I just began to enjoy people. Where once I had been extremely self-centered, I could look at other people and share their joys, their sorrows—pray with them and for them, help where I could. I could not keep inside my desire for them to experience the quality of life I had myself discovered with the Lord. So it became the most natural thing of all to tell people I met about what He had done for us. I discovered myself unbound to speak with and relate to people on a new level. It became a great joy and privilege when I was asked to speak rather than the nightmare any public exposure had been earlier in my life. My former shyness fell away and was replaced by a great love for people. The Lord indeed, one thing at a time, was gradually transforming me, fashioning me into the man He had always intended me to be, but that I could never have become on my own apart from Him.

Such new attitudes represented miracles. I truly was becoming a changed man, from the inside right out to the outside.

And a day at a time, through all the multitude of details in life, Anne and I saw more clearly than ever that God was faithful. We had put our trust in Him and He had never disappointed us. Indeed, He had given us the abundant joy and fulfillment we had been searching for all along. I am not about to tell you any of this was easy. We still have the trials and testings that are present in everyday living in every person's life, but now we know a Lord who loves and cares for us, whom we trust and know to be so very faithful even when we slip and fall.

CHAPTER 22

Becoming One

Characterizing the years after my retirement from running, I think I would use the single word *growth*. As individuals and as a family our roots continued to extend deeper and deeper into the bedrock of God's life within us.

Encouragement has come in many forms, through many people. I remember one such letter from Anne's brother, Tom. "Thanks for the atmosphere of praise that permeates your family. Thanks for your family and just the opportunity to witness a 'real live' and workable Christian family."

Living in the spiritual realm is much like preparing for a race in the physical realm. At one point I'm working on speed, then endurance, then on muscle tone. When not actually running I'm conscious of diet, of rest, and other factors. There are strategies and goals to be considered.

Spiritual growth progresses according to much the same pattern. Every incident I face throughout the day is intended to "train" my spiritual muscles of patience or kindness or reliance on the Lord. The difficulties and trials I continue to encounter teach me endurance' in much the same way a ten-mile run every morning does for my body.

Therefore, once my competitive running days were behind me, I found myself training still, but in a much different way. Now I was developing my mental and emotional and spiritual impulses and reactions, always with the goal of modeling myself after Jesus. We were making headway—ridding ourselves of old attitudes, letting Christ put in His way of thinking and acting.

And that, of course, is the essence of growth, the essence of life itself. That is where the abundant and fulfilling life originates—by

My four children taking a lap at the KU track in 1975.

living according to the example of Jesus. It is a life outside of one's *self,* a life founded in a loving and intimate relationship with God the Father.

Apart from God, I was empty of this primary meaning of life. I had experienced periodic cravings toward "something more," though I didn't know what that craving meant or who was the something more I was in pursuit of.

Anne and I had tried to satisfy these deep longings in our hearts through various externals—running, music, books, food, our intellects, and even our relationship with one another. But of course none of these things filled the hole inside our hearts. Even after we became Christians, to a degree it was a self-centered thing that continued to focus on external factors—hoping to get my running squared away, wanting peace and happiness, seeking an escape from the anxiety and pressure, and so on.

As we have grown with the Lord and as the external incidents of our daily lives "train" us to view life from a spiritual perspective, a new awareness has come upon us of what life, at its foundational core, was intended to be. The cravings within our spirits were not longing after externals at all, not even after such qualities as happiness, joy, peace, or freedom from pressure. Those are simply by-products of something even more fundamental. That's what we ultimately began to see—that the longing of the human heart is toward a deep fellowship with God, a very intimate and personal relationship of communion at the heart level.

If I can draw the analogy, that is the ultimate in the spiritual world—the Olympics of the Spirit. There is no greater race in life to train for than becoming one with the God who created us. That is life's true gold—not bestowed for one brief moment of worldly glory, but a relationship that endures throughout all time. It is toward that relationship with Him, that prized and intimate friendship in the heart, that God is training each one of us. Readying us to receive life's true gold, however, requires that many sharp edges be knocked off our personalities. The higher the prize, the more rigorous must be the training. My favorite piece of Scripture explains this so vivdly: "Do you not know that in a race all the runners run, but only one gets the prize? Run in such a way as to get the prize. Everyone who competes in the games goes into strict training. They do it to get a crown that will not last; but we do it to get a crown that will last forever. Therefore, I do not run like a man running aimlessly; I do not fight like a man beating the air. No, I beat my body and make it my slave so that after I have preached to others, I myself will not be disqualified for the prize (1 Corinthians 9:24–27, NIV).

One night Anne and I were lying in bed talking, as we often do, conversing back and forth about everything that had been happening in our lives and all the truths the Lord was showing us.

At one point Anne turned to me and said, "I love Jesus more than I love you."

Wham! I felt like I'd been socked in the belly with a baseball bat.

What a devastating thing to hear! From my wife, who loved me and had stood by me through thick and thin. The pain must have shown all over my face.

Yet once I recovered and could see what Anne really meant, it proved such a realization of where we as a couple were headed. We were moving into a love relationship with the Lord of our lives. Once I got my wind back, after the initial shock, I could see that her words represented my heart's attitude as well. We were becoming one just as the Bible said we were meant to be, fitting our strengths and weaknesses together to make a whole. We had grown to the point where we loved the Lord with *all* our hearts, *all* our souls, *all*

The Ryun tradition carries on as all four of our children participate in the
AAU Junior Olympics.

our minds, and *all* our strength. And nothing—not even each other
—could ever take the place of God being first in our lives.

Talking later about the parallels between athletics and the
spiritual life, Anne commented in her casual manner with laughter
interspersed, "It's really special how the Lord was really preparing
you for a life with Him all along, especially through your running."

"Nothing in life ever happens by accident," I said. "I'm sure the
discipline of all those early morning runs makes it easier now to get
up early to spend time with the Lord every day."

"And all the verses in the Bible equating the Christian life with
a race—'Run the good race . . . press on toward the prize . . . run
with patience the race that is set before us . . . all the runners run
the race, but only one wins the prize.' "

The race—the spiritual adventure—we are now involved in in-
volves our whole family and every facet of our relationship together. Everywhere our spiritual horizons are being expanded. We
are mapping our own destinies in Christ Jesus. We are in the hold
of God's Spirit, moving with Him wherever He takes us.

"You know," I said one day, "I really did win the gold after all."

"How do you mean?" asked Anne with a puzzled look on her
face.

The entire Ryun family in Santa Barbara in 1979.

"The gold isn't a medal. That's just a hunk of ore someone dug out of the ground. The real ultimate in life, the highest victory of all, is a deepening friendship with Jesus. He's given us that without holding back a thing!"

"You're right! And I've got the gold too. That's a real riot—me a gold medalist!"

"The wonderful thing about the Lord is that He wants to give it to *everybody!* That's going to be a crowded victory stand some-day. Because those who know the Lord are all winners! He wants to give everyone the intimacy and the strength and toughness of His love."

Contrary to what might at first seem to be the case, our deepening personal relationships with the Lord has strengthened the love Anne and I have for one another and has cemented our family ties all the tighter. In God's economy, increased love in one direction does not detract from love in any other direction but adds to it. Love for the Lord has increased our capacity to love all others. It has opened us up, freed us to be all that God has made us to be.

Therefore Anne and I find ourselves loving and knowing one another in deeper and more exciting ways all the time. We have always been best friends. Now it is a three-way friendship, which has added immeasurably to its depth and richness.

One day Anne and I went out from the back of our home in Lawrence, Kansas, and walked up through the tall grass onto the hill overlooking the valley. There was a warm, sweet breeze blowing from the south. We could hear the cows in the neighboring field mooing peacefully. We walked, hand in hand, all the way to the top, mostly in silence as we found ourselves caught in the reminiscences of our years together.

"The children will be home soon," Anne said at last. "I think I saw the bus winding its way there a moment ago."

I looked where she was pointing but it was now hidden from view.

"I know," I said. "I promised Ned and Drew a game of soccer up here in the field today, and Catharine a game of chess."

"Fitting all that in before dinner will be some trick," laughed Anne.

Neither of us spoke for a moment.

"They're precious children of the Lord, aren't they?" I said.

Anne said nothing. When I looked over at her, she was crying softly.

"Yes, they are," she said finally, through the tears. "The Lord continues to be so good to us, Jim. I wouldn't trade the life I've had with you and with Him for anything."

Drawn as if by common consent, we turned and began slowly making our descent toward the house. The bus still wasn't visible, but I could hear the rumbling of its diesel motor as it approached.

From where we stood, on a clear night, the lights of Topeka and Kansas City could barely be seen. Lawrence lay spread out in the valley before us, some eight miles distant. That was where so much of it had happened. I swung my head around to take in the scene, thinking of my days of running down in that valley below and of the events of the years since. Anne's mind had apparently been on the same wavelength.

Halfway down the hill she said, as if summarizing our lives together, "I praise the Lord that Jesus has never given up on us and continues to mold us into His image."

I sighed deeply, looked at Anne with a smile, and nodded. There were no other words that needed to be spoken.

The bus had arrived and the far-off happy sounds of four children running up the road greeted us.

Index